OUR
WOODLAND
TREASURES

OUR WOODLAND TREASURES

Peaceful, Startling,
Rambunctious & Amazing
Animals & Plants

nature essays by

MIRIAM SANDERS

MEADS MOUNTAIN PRESS
WOODSTOCK, NEW YORK
AND

Station Hill Press

BARRYTOWN, NEW YORK

Published by Station Hill Press, the publishing project of the Institute for Publishing Arts, Inc., 120 Station Hill Road, Barrytown, NY 12507, New York, a not-for-profit, tax-exempt organization [501(c)(3)], and Meads Mountain Press, PO Box 729, Woodstock, NY, 12498.

Online catalogue: www.stationhill.org
e-mail: publishers@stationhill.org
Cover painting and interior illustrations by Miriam Sanders.
Cover and interior design by Susan Quasha.
Photograph of author by Olivia Twine.

Library of Congress Cataloging-in-Publication Data

Names: Sanders, Miriam, author.
Title: Our woodland treasures : peaceful, startling, rambunctious & amazing
   animals & plants : nature essays / by Miriam Sanders.
Description: Barrytown, New York : Station Hill Press, 2020.
Identifiers: LCCN 2019050543 | ISBN 9781581771923 (paperback)
Subjects: LCSH: Natural history—Miscellanea.
Classification: LCC QH45.5 .S26 2020 | DDC 508—dc23
LC record available at https://lccn.loc.gov/2019050543

Manufactured in the United States of America.

Contents

An Elfin Visitor in the Kitchen   (The Flying Squirrel)   1

A Fearless Fellow in Evening Attire   (The Skunk)   3

Dragons, Damsels and Ogres at the Pond   (The Dragonfly)   5

The Mouse-Eared One Who Flees the Light   (The Brown Bat)   8

Enchantments of a Midsummer Evening   (Fireflies)   10

A Fantastic Feathered Jewel   (The Hummingbird)   13

Our National Bird?   (The Turkey)   15

Named by the Native Americans "Little Brother"   (The Beaver)   17

A Life on the Run   (The Eastern Cottontail)   19

A Woodland Sprite   (The White-Footed Mouse)   23

The Glory of Our Native Sugar Maple   25

Hymn to Maple Syrup   27

The Gallant Canada Goose   33

A Scarlet Bloom in the Bare Winter Bush   (The Cardinal)   35

The Amazing Opossum—A Living Fossil   37

The Smartest Dog of All   (The Fox)   39

The Woodchuck—A Master Engineer   42

Plaintive Cries in the Night   (The Screech Owl)   45

An Amiable Creature Clad in Armor   (The Eastern Box Turtle)   48

Rhapsody in Blue   (The Eastern Blue Bird)   50

A Gentle Reminder   (The Mourning Dove)   52

An Ancient Friend   (The Mallard)   54

The Humble-Bee   (The Bumblebee)   56

Wildcat of the Woods   (The Bobcat)   58

The Misunderstood Mole—A Warrior in Black Velvet   60

A Crimson Hunter in the Wet Green Grass   (The Red Eft)   62

A Striped Beguiler   (The Chipmunk)   64

Endless Toil for the Good of All   (The Honey Bee)   68

Wild Canary of the Wayside   (The Goldfinch)   71

A Miraculous Monarch   (Monarch Butterfly)   73

At the Edge of a Parking Lot   76

Watchman of the Woods   (The Eastern Crow)   78

The Dying Crow   82

There are Giants in Our Hills   (The Black Bear)   84

A Planter of Oak Forests   (The Eastern Blue Jay)   87

The Return of the Red Army   (The Ladybug)   89

A Furry Forecaster of Winter's Weather   (The Woolly Bear)   91

Mischief in a Mask   (The Raccoon)   93

A Gentle Creature Fiercely Armed   (The Porcupine)   96

The Mysterious Mistletoe   99

A Diminutive Despot   (The Red Squirrel)   101

An Invasion of Voles   104

The Courageous Chickadee   107

The Giant Mouse   (The Muskrat)   110

Return of the Redwings   (The Red-Winged Blackbird)   113

The Mayapple   115

A Congenial Garden Companion   (The Toad)   117

The Glorious Northern Oriole   120

The Devoted Rock Dove   123

The Great Egret   126

A Woodland Majesty   (The White-Tailed Buck)   129

A Most Impressive Woodpecker   132

A Giant Under Siege   (The Eastern Hemlock)   134

A Spectral Presence   (The Barn Owl)   136

Until Death Do They Part   (The Lichen)   138

A Brown Velvet Beauty in the Marsh   (The Cattail)   141

A Dainty Vampire   (The Mosquito)   144

A Glorious Grosbeak   146

An Enticing Roadside Beauty   (The Milkweed)   148

A Twig with Legs   (The Walking Stick)   151

Our Good Friend Downy   (The Woodpecker)   153

There Are Tigers in the Flower Beds!   (The Eastern Tiger
    Swallowtail)   155

A Singing Cat in the Hedgerow   (The Catbird)   157

The Glorious American Chestnut Shall Arise Once Again!   159

Australian Nomads Camp in the Livingroom!   (The Budgerigar)   163

The Exquisite Wood Duck   166

A Reckless Debauch   (The Hellbender)   169

A Tiny Woodland Acrobat   (The Nuthatch)   172

The Return of the Mountain Lion   175

The Insatiable Short-Tailed Shrew   178

The Shy Serpent of Overlook Mountain   (The Rattlesnake)   180

A Startling Beauty   (The Cecropia)   185

The Beautiful Bird From the West Who Came to Stay
    (The House Finch)   187

A Haunting Call in the Gloaming   (The Whip-Poor Will)   189

Ghostly Flowers of the Shaded Forest Floor   (The Indian Pipe)   191

The Skydancer   (The American Woodcock)   193

Coyote the Trickster   196

The Snowbirds Return!   (The Juncos)   199

Smallest Songsters of Springtime   (Spring Peepers)   201

A Planter of Forests   (The Eastern Gray Squirrel)   205

Lost and Gone Forever   (The Carolina Parakeet)   208

ABOUT THE AUTHOR   211

About

OUR WOODLAND TREASURES

When Miriam and I, with the help of Woodstocker Alan Sussman, started publishing *The Woodstock Journal* in 1995, Miriam began a weekly nature column which became an astounding success, with a good number of readers turning first to Miriam's remarkable columns. For the next eight years Miriam published her essays in every issue. Here are eighty of them, in all their beauty and glory.

—Ed Sanders

AN ELFIN VISITOR
in the KITCHEN

Several nights ago, when I was unable to sleep, I decided to sit at the kitchen table and read, so as not to waken my husband, Edward. It was quite late, three o'clock A.M. to be exact, when I became aware of a rustling sound over the kitchen window, above the sink. "Probably a white-footed mouse," I thought, and decided to ignore it. The rustling was soon accompanied by a determined chewing sound that I realized was of the Chinese bamboo vegetable steamer, which hangs from a nail over the sink, being eaten. Reluctantly, I put down my book and went over to chastise the little visitor. As I approached, I realized that I was not seeing a mouse, but a somewhat larger creature perched upon the rim of the steamer. I wondered if it were an endangered woodrat. Then I saw the wide fluffy tail. Huge, glistening black eyes regarded me fearlessly as the little animal ate the bamboo. Its fur was a soft, reddish-brown on the tail, head, and back, and its stomach and throat were white. There were loose folds of fur-covered skin along its sides. Suddenly, I knew that I was facing a creature I had only seen before in pictures. It was a flying squirrel!

I called softly to Edward to come quickly and quietly and see what was in the kitchen, but, as he approached, the squirrel leaped agilely to an aperture leading to the attic and disappeared. Grumbling, Edward returned to bed, and the squirrel hopped down again to eat his steamer.

I was thrilled to be in the presence of this elfin creature, which is rarely encountered except by woodsmen who fell trees. Although it may gain access to an attic, this squirrel makes its nest in a woodpecker's hollow, in what is known as a "snag": a standing dead tree.

It is unfortunate that many forests are managed in such a way that tree snags are systematically removed, since the cavities carved in them by woodpeckers are in great demand as nesting sites for birds as well as mammals.

The flying squirrel is almost entirely nocturnal. Its extremely large eyes and its "baby-face" make it look like a child's toy. The loose folds of furred skin I had noticed on the sides of our little visitor extend from the wrists of its forelegs to the ankles of its hindlegs, making flaps. When these flaps are extended, they enable the squirrel to glide as much as one hundred and fifty feet!

The flying squirrel eats nuts, fruits, sugar maple buds, and insects. It greatly enjoys eating pine cone seeds, and makes nighttime visits to bird feeders as well. However, it is quite opportunistic, and may snatch a drowsy roosting bird, or eat an occasional fledgling or egg.

The breeding season for northern flying squirrels is in February and March. The helpless, pink babies, generally three or four in number, are usually born in a tree cavity. The nest is lined with soft wood fibers and fur plucked from the mother's breast. She spreads her "wing" flaps over the babies to keep them warm. The babies are fully furred in two weeks, and their eyes and ears are open in four. The flying squirrel mother is extremely attentive to her young, rarely leaving them for more than a few moments to obtain food.

I was very sorry that Edward had not witnessed the visit of that most dainty and beautiful of squirrels, a true woodland spirit, the flying squirrel.

A FEARLESS FELLOW
in EVENING ATTIRE

In his glossy black fur trimmed with gleaming white stripes, the skunk looks like a portly gentleman in evening clothes as he walks slowly across the road in the moonlight. His wonderful plumey tail, rivaling that of the fox, is carried slightly aloft. The skunk's front legs are much shorter than his back legs, giving him a peculiar waddling gait. His front feet possess powerful claws with which he digs a den, although he may be quite happy to utilize an abandoned woodchuck's burrow, or even to make his home beneath a building.

The skunk enjoys eating fruits and berries, insects, small mammals, snakes and frogs. It also eats the eggs and fledgelings of birds that nest upon the ground. Paradoxically, although the skunk is of great benefit to farmers, in that, when it burrows under barns it will rid them of unwanted rodents, it will also try to eat the poultry! In the summer, the skunk's diet consists primarily of insects, and it destroys great numbers of injurious ones, especially grasshoppers, beetles, cutworms and grubs. However, the skunk also relishes honeybees. It scratches the front of the hives until the bees swarm out angrily, then stamps on them and eats them!

Skunk babies are born in the late spring—deaf and blind, wrinkled and almost hairless, the black and white pattern already apparent on their skin. After about five weeks, they are fully-furred and weaned. They can be seen out on hunting expeditions with their mother, trailing single-file after her in the moonlight.

The following winter, the skunk family retreats to the den and sleeps through the coldest weather. By mid-February, male skunks may be seen abroad in search of amour.

The skunk is an intelligent creature, fearless and dignified. It actually has a very amiable disposition, however, when it feels threatened, it will utilize its great weapon of self-defense. First, the skunk warns the enemy by stamping its front feet, and, perhaps, emitting a low growl. Next, it lifts its beautiful tail high, and spreads the fur. It bends its body into a "U" shape so that its face and rear both point at the enemy, and it can see where it is aiming its weaponry. Then, from two glands at the base of the tail, it shoots a sulfurous compound with great accuracy. This spray is quite painful if it hits the eyes, causing copious tearing but no permanent blindness. The odor of the spray may be perceived for a distance of more than a mile. According to Audobon's colleague, the Reverend John Bachman, the skunk's spray is luminous in the dark, like "an attenuated stream of phosphoric light." Not everyone finds the skunk's spray to be offensive. The naturalist John Burroughs wrote of it, "It approaches the sublime, and makes the nose tingle.... It is tonic and bracing, and I can readily believe has rare medicinal qualities."

Skunks are gentle and easily tamed, and it is claimed that they are more affectionate and attentive than cats. When descented, they are said to make excellent pets.

DRAGONS, DAMSELS *and* OGRES
at the POND

What a pleasing sight it is on a summer's day, to see beautiful dragonflies flitting over the pond on iridescent wings, their long slender bodies gleaming in the sunlight.

The insects' four large wings, gauzy and shimmering, are actually quite powerful. They can move independently, allowing dragonflies to fly forward and backward, attaining a speed of sixty miles per hour when pursuing prey or eluding a bird.

The dragonfly is a consummate predator, with a head that can move in all directions, almost covered by enormous compound eyes. Although the dragonfly cannot walk on its long legs, it can perch on a twig. It can hold these spiny legs together to form a basket, and catch insects in it as it flies! Many mosquitoes, hovering over ponds to lay eggs, are caught in this manner.

Damselflies, the smaller cousins of the dragonfly, are more slender and delicate, their bodies even brighter-hued. When they rest, most fold their wings over their backs, as do butterflies. (Dragonflies spread their wings when at rest.)

There's a very handsome damselfly commonly encountered in Woodstock known as the black-winged damselfly. Its velvetly black wings contrast beautifully with its metallic-turquoise body. Among the many small insects consumed by this damselfly are harmful aphids.

Male and female dragonflies and damselflies often fly together over water, mating in the air. Some species allow their eggs to fall into the water, some place the eggs on aquatic plants, and some actually pierce the stems of these plants and place the eggs within.

The true "ogres" of the pond are the dragonfly young, known as nymphs or naiads. These creatures are generally muddy in color, and coated with muddy particles for camouflage.

The naiad has a huge lower lip that folds back over its face like a mask. The tip of this lip is covered with hooks and barbs. When the naiad senses prey, it shoots the huge lip forward and impales the victim, then draws it to its mouth and devours it. In this way, it consumes enormous numbers of aquatic insects such as mosquito wigglers, and worms, tadpoles and tiny fish as well.

The naiad, eating steadily, undergoes several growing stages and molts. Finally, emerging from the water, it crawls up the stem of an aquatic plant, or onto a rock, splits it skin, and a perfectly formed adult dragonfly emerges.

Dragonflies have an ancient lineage; the fossil record shows that their relatives existed 300 million years ago. Some of these early dragonflies were huge, with a wingspread of two and a half feet!

THE MOUSE-EARED ONE
WHO FLEES *the* LIGHT

Look up at the sky this evening, just at dusk, and you may be rewarded by the sight of little brown bats flitting over the treetops. They dart quickly and erratically in their hungry search for mosquitoes and other night-flying insects.

In order to avoid obstacles and locate prey, the bat uses a system of echolocation. It emits pulses of sound that strike objects and return as echoes. By interpreting these echoes, the bat can discern the shape of an object, its location and how fast it is moving. According to Bat Conservation International, a single bat can capture and consume as many as 600 insects in one hour!

Residents of the Chautauqua summer resort in upstate New York have encouraged bats to live there for more than 50 years, as an alternative to pesticide use for mosquito control. Besides mosquitoes, bats eat agricultural pests such as corn borers, grain and cutworm moths, potato beetles and grasshoppers.

The little brown bat, also known as *myotis lucifugens*, or, "the mouse-eared one who flees the light," is an insect-eating species frequently encountered in this area. It is a tiny creature, barely weighing half an ounce. Its body, covered with soft, dark brown fur, is three and a half inches long from head to tail tip, and its wing span is ten inches.

This is a social bat, often forming summer colonies in attics, barns, caves, cliff faces and even walls of older buildings. These colonies may consist of up to several hundred individuals.

In winter, little brown bats hibernate, often grouping in caves or mines, where their rate of breathing may fall to only once every five minutes.

A little brown bat may live more than twenty years, devouring prodigious numbers of insects each summer.

Remember, never touch a downed bat, because of the possibility, although remote, that it may have rabies; and vaccinate your animals against rabies BEFORE they encounter wildlife.

ENCHANTMENTS
of a MIDSUMMER EVENING

I magine the joy and wonder of a city child when he first sees fireflies. Their tiny sparks of light dancing over a meadow, a creek, or at the edge of a wood at dusk seem magical.

Fireflies are actually small, slender, soft-bodied beetles. They have special cells at the tip of their abdomens that are supplied with air tubes. Through these tubes, oxygen for the light-producing process is obtained.

Fireflies flash their lights to attract a mate. The male flashes as he flies; the female flashes a matching signal near the ground where she rests. The male draws closer and closer as they exchange signals until they meet and mate.

After mating, the female firefly lays her eggs on the moist ground or under damp debris. The larvae which emerge are nocturnal, carnivorous and luminous.

Countless children, and many adults as well, have collected fireflies, put them in a jar, and enjoyed the light show!

Another creature of the night that makes a lasting impression on those who see it for the first time is the majestic luna moth. This beautiful moth belongs to the family of Giant Silkworm Moths. Its elegant apple-green wings have a span of four and a half inches. The front wings are edged with rosy purple and have "eye-spots." The hind wings also have "eye-spots" and very long graceful swallow tails. The body is covered with white fur as are the inner edges of the hind wings.

The large green caterpillar feeds on the leaves of hickory, birch and many other trees. It usually spins its thin papery cocoon, a silken thread around its body, then wraps itself in a leaf, amidst leaves on the ground.

The luna moth is sometimes seen fluttering around a street light, resembling a bat from afar, or, clinging to a window screen. Don't attempt to capture this wonderful creature, because, unfortunately, it is now endangered due to pesticides and pollution.

A FANTASTIC FEATHERED JEWEL

No scene in the tropical rain forest is more exquisite than the sight of our hummingbird, a ruby at his throat, sipping nectar from our native bee-balm, its scarlet petals glowing in the sun.

This tiniest of birds possesses the most brilliant iridescent plumage. His head, shoulders and back gleam with a burnished metallic green lustre.

The name "hummingbird" derives from the humming sound that the bird's wings make in flight. These powerful wings trace a figure eight in the air as the bird hovers, but they appear as a blur to the human eye. That is because they beat more than fifty times per second! Hummingbirds are among the fastest birds. Not only can they hover, they can fly up, down, forward and even backward.

The tiny ruby-throated hummingbird, less than four inches in length, must fly almost two thousand miles when it leaves the Eastern United States to spend the winter months in Central America. Its return flight is timed to coincide with the flowering of its food plants.

The hummingbird is particularly attracted to tubular red flowers, such as those of salvia, trumpet creeper, bee-balm and azalea. It feeds from many others, such as petunia, jewelweed and thistle. The bird has a thin, long, pointed beak, perfectly shaped to insert into the corolla of these flowers. The tongue within is shaped like a tube with which it sucks up nectar. Small insects are retrieved as well. As the hummingbird moves from flower to flower, it pollinates them.

The hummingbird's nest, found in a forest clearing, is a tiny deep cup, about the size of half a walnut. It looks as dainty as if it were made by fairies, but it is quite sturdy. It is fashioned of soft plant fibers, woven with spider web silk, lined with down and decorated with bits of lichen. It looks just like part of the branch to which it is attached. Within the nest, there are never more than two pea-sized white eggs. The mother bird incubates these eggs for sixteen days, then, she alone rears the chicks.

Our hummingbirds lead a precarious existence. They have been caught by dragonflies, praying mantises and frogs, trapped in spider webs, and even stuck to thistles!

OUR NATIONAL BIRD?

Have you seen the large number of turkeys prancing single file through Woodstock yards this summer? There is one flock consisting of two mothers and fourteen babies that appears each afternoon on our front lawn.

Turkeys are such droll, comical creatures that I can't help but laugh when I see them, and throw them an occasional handful of corn. Of course, this causes great excitement—much clucking, gobble-gobbling, and an occasional feather flying as they vie for the golden treat.

The turkey's natural food is largely vegetable matter, mostly seeds. They vastly enjoy acorns and beechnuts. They eat a wide variety of insects, especially grasshoppers, and small crustaceans, amphibians and reptiles are also consumed.

Wild turkeys are magnificent large birds, the male reaching a weight of twenty-two pounds and the female about half as much. The plumage is splendid. The feathers are deep brown with brilliant green, bronze and copper metallic reflections. The male has a long tassel of black bristles on his upper breast that juts forward when he displays.

Both male and female have heads and necks that are naked and ornamented with warty tubercules. The color of these ornaments may be red, blue or white according to the bird's mood. In the spring and summer, the male turkeys' head and neck are predominantly red.

The male and female bird both have a hanging fold beneath the throat called a wattle. The male also has a long pendulous growth of flesh that hangs over his beak called a caruncle or snood. When the bird is angry the snood and wattle swell and redden.

Turkeys are polygamous. The male struts about displaying his beautiful feathers and "gobbling" aggressively to attract a harem.

He protrudes his chest, raises his iridescent neck feathers like a ruff, lowers his wings till their tips scrape the ground, and spreads his tail like a large fan. The hens approach only when they are willing.

A single mating produces ten to fifteen pale brown eggs, lightly speckled with brown and black. The nest is built in a shallow depression in the forest floor, lined with leaves and well concealed beneath vegetation. The hen sits on her eggs for twenty-eight days. Although the babies are feathered when hatched, and can soon run about, they are quite delicate during the first six weeks of life.

Turkeys are strong fliers, but only for a distance of about a quarter of a mile. When danger threatens, they tend to run rather than fly. At night, they roost high in the tree tops.

The wild turkey, *Meleagris gallopavo*, is found from New York to Colorado and south to northern Mexico. The Native Americans of Mexico domesticated it, and the Spanish Conquistadors brought it to Europe in the 16th century. It was almost hunted to extinction, but, due to careful reintroduction, it is once again fairly common in many parts of its former range.

NAMED BY *the* NATIVES
"LITTLE BROTHER"

Our native beaver, *castor canadensis*, is a large, chubby, pleasant rodent, whose family is closely related to that of the squirrel. It measures two and a half feet in length from its nose to its tail. The large, flat, scaly tail is about ten inches long, and is used as a rudder. When the beaver slaps his tail down hard on the water, it is the traditional signal of danger. A fully grown beaver can weigh over forty pounds, mate for life, and live thirty years!

The front surface of the beaver's teeth is covered with tough orange enamel. The back of the teeth is soft and wears down more quickly, forming a sharp chisel edge. With these strong teeth, the beaver can fell trees, gnaw off branches, and strip and eat the tasty green inner bark. Willow, birch, poplar and aspen are favored food, and water lilies and berries are greatly enjoyed.

By damming small streams, beavers form ponds that provide deep enough water to build their homes, called lodges. Beavers are sociable and communally cooperative. Colonies of beavers work together in building dams. They fell trees near the water's edge, cut them into pieces, and float them into place. The beavers weave a solid layer of branches and small trunks. They fill it in with mud and stones for strength. Sometimes green shoots take root, forming a hedge.

When there are desirable trees inland, beavers dig canals to reach them. Then they float the branches through the canals and back to the pond.

The beaver's lodge is a large dome built in a pond, with its living chambers above the water line. The entrance lies beneath the water's surface. The walls are made of branches and plastered over with mud. (Although the beaver's hind feet are fully webbed, its forefeet are used like hands. It carries mud pressed against its breast with the forefeet, and plasters with them as well.)

In the autumn, the beavers try to become as fat as possible to sustain themselves in the coming winter's cold. They lay in stores of branches underwater beneath the lodges. They plaster the lodges with fresh mud, which, upon freezing, becomes as hard as stone. The lodges provide warm, weatherproof homes, safe from hungry predators.

In the spring, when the ice melts, and the weeds grow again, the baby beavers called "kits" are born. They are fully furred, with open eyes. They mature slowly. The parents teach them to swim and dive, and where danger lies. When the young beavers are two years old, they are driven away so that the new babies will have a better chance for survival.

Beavers have been relentlessly pursued for their valuable fur. While the outer fur is coarse and reddish-brown, the greyish inner fur is very dense, silky and smooth. The early settlers in North America prized the thick fur of beavers for warm coats and hats. Trappers killed beavers by the millions and made fortunes. The trade in beaver skins helped spur the conquest of the West.

The beaver is a great conservationist. By damming small streams to form ponds, beavers make the water from heavy rains and melting snow run off much more slowly than it otherwise would. After the mass killing of beavers, there were few left to build dams. Water flowed rapidly down streams eroding away much good soil, and causing floods in the lands below. The land that was ruined had had a much greater value than the value of the beaver skins.

When streams are held in by beaver dams, the water is stilled and algae builds up. A special pond ecosystem is created. Food is provided for invertebrates, fish, frogs, turtles and snakes. Raccoons and herons visit the pond, and swans, geese and ducks make nests there. When big trees are felled, young saplings and weeds spring up providing food for deer. The pond eventually fills in, and there is good rich soil in place of a rocky riverbed.

A LIFE *on the* RUN

The Eastern Cottontail

W ell into the 20th century, rabbits were considered to be rodents. Today, based on certain physical differences from the *Rodentia*, rabbits are classified in a very small family called *Lagomorpha*. This family consists only of pikas, rabbits, and hares. Rabbits and rodents have long, curved, continuously growing incisor teeth for gnawing. Rabbits have two small, extra incisors behind the large visible incisors in the upper jaw.

In the summer, rabbits eat many juicy leaves, grasses, herbs, flowers, and fruits; in the winter they switch over to bark, twigs, buds, and evergreen needles. They will even search for fallen seeds beneath birdfeeders.

The rabbit's wonderfully long ears, which are laid back side to side when it is at rest, can stand straight up when it needs to hear what is approaching. If it is alarmed, the rabbit will sit up high on its haunches, wiggle its nose to catch every scent, and perk up the funnel-shaped ears, which can be moved independently. The rabbit's eyes, set on the sides of its head, give a wide field of vision. The soft, silky fur, grayish-brown in color, helps our cottontail hide from its enemies. It will sometimes "freeze," and then be very hard to see amidst leaves and trees. If the rabbit must run to escape, its strong hind legs allow it to make huge jumps, eight feet or more in length. As it runs, the fluffy, white, powder-puff tail flashes a warning signal.

Sometimes, courting rabbits can be seen playing a strange game in the moonlight. A pair will face one another, one will leap into the air, and the other will run underneath it!

Our eastern cottontail does not go down a "rabbit hole" as does the rabbit in Alice in Wonderland.

It makes its nest, called a "form," in a shallow depression under grasses, a brush pile, or perhaps, in a briar patch. If the weather is very severe, the rabbit may seek shelter in an old woodchuck or skunk burrow.

A mother rabbit lines the nest with fur plucked from her own breast, and covers the babies with a blanket made of fur and soft grasses. The five or six rabbit babies are born almost naked and blind, unlike their cousins the hares, which are born fully furred and with open eyes.

Historically, the rabbit family has been viewed very differently in various cultures. The Native American Algonquins believed that the Great Hare, Michabo, created the earth, water, and fish, and reestablished the earth after The Flood. The domesticated rabbit, a European species, is a very important laboratory animal. On the other hand, when the same European rabbit was introduced to Australia and New Zealand, it had few natural enemies and became a scourge.

Our cottontail is beset by enemies. It is preyed upon by human hunters, foxes, weasels, dogs, cats, owls, eagles, hawks, crows, and snakes. That it manages to survive at all is due to its adaptability, agility, fecundity and timidity.

A WOODLAND SPRITE

Our native white-footed mouse, *Peromyscus leucopus*, differs considerably from its urban cousin, the house mouse, both in appearance and in demeanor.

Our white-foot is one of the most beautiful of mammals. When a juvenile, it is a soft gray and white in color, but, as an adult, its fur is golden-brown on its back, and white on the throat, stomach, and feet. The ears are large, the eyes are huge and shiny-black, and the tail is furred: brown above and white beneath.

While the house mouse is furtive, our white-foot is bold and inquisitive. It is apt to pop out from some cranny and scrutinize you, as if it were wondering, "Who is this large creature sharing my warm, hollow tree?"

Unlike the house mouse, the white-foot is bodily clean. It licks and grooms itself often, and washes its face each time that it eats.

White-footed mice prefer to eat nuts, seeds, berries, grasses, herbs, and insects. They work very hard carrying this food in their cheek pouches, as do hamsters and chipmunks, in order to store it in hoards for winter use. Sometimes, one finds these hoards in the oddest of places, such as in the toes of infrequently worn shoes!

The mother white-foot is a model of devotion. She builds a nest of the softest materials available, such as, grasses, rags or cotton, and fluffs them with her mouth and paws. The babies are born naked and pink, unable to see or hear. The mother mouse hovers over them to keep them warm, only leaving the nest briefly to get food.

There are many antique references as to the white-footed mouse singing sweetly as a bird. For example, one Mr. Hiskey, in an early 20th century issue of American Naturalist stated, "I was sitting..... not far from a half-open closet door, when I was startled by a sound issuing from the closet, of such marvelous beauty that I at once asked my wife how 'Bobbie Burns' (our canary) had found his way into the closet, and what could start him to singing such a queer and sweet song in the dark. I procured a light and found it to be a mouse!.... His song was not a chirp, but a continuous song of a musical tone, quite varied in pitch."

A white-footed mouse does not hibernate, but is active all winter long. Moonlit nights with snow on the ground are especially dangerous times for this tiny creature preyed upon by so many. One winter, I had a white-foot as a temporary pet. She had been quite rambunctious, running noisily about the kitchen, getting into foodstuffs, and gnawing loudly. I caught her in a live trap, but I didn't have the heart to put her out in the bitter cold without her hoard of food. I placed her in an aquarium, furnished, as for any small rodent, with a nest-box. One day, I couldn't believe what I was seeing; there were two mice at the food dish, then three, four, five! The mother mouse had given birth in the privacy of her nest-box. The mouse family was quite companiable. The babies enjoyed playing together, grooming one another, and running in their little wheels. It was only with great reluctance that I set them all free in the spring.

THE GLORY *of our* NATIVE
SUGAR MAPLE

Now that their fiery-hued leaves have fallen, the autumn splendor of our sugar maples becomes a memory. The sugar maple, also known as *Acer saccharum*, rock or hard maple, is a magnificent tree; not only beautiful to look at, it provides us with wonderful gifts year round.

Sugar maple wood is pale, becoming rosy with exposure to light. It is strong, tough and fine-grained, and when polished has a silky lustre.

The timber is used for such diverse things as the interior finish of houses, flooring, boats, furniture, saddles, tool handles, and the action of pianos. Occasionally, sugar maple wood shows a curly grain or a spotted grain which is known as "birds-eye maple." These woods are considered to be very ornamental and are much sought after.

In the summer, the sugar maple provides excellent shade. It has many branches closely set at sharp angles to the trunk. The leaves, arranged in a dense, overlapping pattern, are deep green above, pale green beneath. In optimum conditions, this stately tree may rise to over one hundred twenty feet in height!

In the fall, the twin-winged seeds twirl down. The green of the leaves gives way to bright crimson red, then orange, then yellow. The explanation for this process is as follows:

There is a layer of cells that lies between the leaf and the stem known as the "abscission layer." The combination of shorter day lengths and cooler nights activates these cells and they cut off the leaf from the stem, depriving it of water and minerals. This causes the green chlorophyll pigment to break down. The abscission layer also prevents the leaf from transporting its sugar to the stem, and the sugar is converted to anthocyanin, a red pigment. Anthocyanin then breaks down, revealing yellow pigments.

The layer of fallen leaves creates a carpet of mulch, which turns into humus that replenishes the soil with nutrients.

For winter heating, only hickory outranks maple as a fuel. Maple ashes yield much potash and alkali. Fresh unleached hard maple ashes make an excellent fertilizer for vegetable gardens. In the spring, the maple gives us its special gift—the delicious sweet sap. Ideal sugaring weathering consists of warm days with freezing nights. This change in temperature between day and night acts as a pump and causes the sap to rise and fall in the tree. The first run of sap is considered to be the best.

The Native Americans made maple syrup in the following manner: Diagonal gashes were made in the trees, and spiles (hollow tubes of hardwood) were inserted beneath the cuts through which sap dripped into bark containers placed on the ground. The collected sap was poured into bark buckets and emptied into large mooseskin containers. These were then pulled on sleds to the place where the sap was boiled all night in hollowed-out log troughs until reduced to syrup. When the syrup became thick, it was stirred with maple-wood paddles until it granulated; sometimes it was poured into molds. Maple syrup was used by the Native Americans to season fruits, vegetables, cereals, and even fish and meat! It was often given as a gift, and was a standard item of trade.

Native American children, and later the settlers' children, greatly enjoyed the sugar-making process. They took particular delight in eating a confection made by pouring hot, thick syrup onto the fresh snow.

Unfortunately, air pollution causing acid rain and acid snow has begun to take its toll on these noble trees. There are many documented cases of crown die-back among the sugar maples. Trees which are stressed are more susceptible to disease, drought, insect infestation, temperature extremes and high winds. Many scientists believe that if environmental detriments continue unabated, our great-grandchildren will not be able to enjoy the presence of sugar maples in the Catskills.

HYMN *to* MAPLE SYRUP

(My husband Edward wrote this poem celebrating our making of maple syrup.)

My pockets are cold with short metal tubes called spiles
with a knob-like protuberance on each upper edge
to keep the buckets from falling off.

I feel affection for the rough swirls of ancient maple bark
for each giant sugar is a Patting Tree

and sometimes I stop to hug a maple as huge
as two people reaching around it,
sliding my arms past spile scars of seasons past,
dark circles in dark crusts
the winter mittens touch,

and then to lean with brace & bit
the knob of it pressing the chest,
and chew through the gray to the butter-tan wood.

The wood-curls at the hole's mouth turn moist
as soon as I screw out the drill bit

Then gently to tap the spile in the hole
& the sap runs shiny out of the shiny tip

Across the creek is an open front sapping shed
with an old Norge stove once gas, but now
outfitted for wood

The correct beatnik hour for emptying
the sap bags is 2 A.M.

Back & forth th' galoshes skwonch scaring the deer
from the yew-berry bush

I rotate the pan on its spile
and pour the sap in a metal pail
then walk through the dark
to the 40-gallon holding can by the shed

steady steady
trying to keep the sap from sloshing
with little frothy waves
to douse the knuckles and gloves
as cold as the ocean at Gloucester.

It's a fine aerobic sapper's trudge
a fourth of a mile or more
tree to can to tree to can
till all of the buckets are empty again.

There's a long rectangular pan with handles
above the fiery stove
I pour a few gallons to fill it.

I love to boil at night,
keeping the Norge's door wide open
and stuffed with overlength wood.
The first rush is sweetest and best

they say, and so it is tonight
as the room width fills
with billows of paradise steam.

Tending the boil I sit out there on
an old oak school desk-chair
working on poems or tales
pausing to flick the shiny skuz
that roils to the top of the pan
to a corner with a slotted spoon

It takes about an hour
to boil away a pan
You learn how to tell how close it is
dipping a spoon for a taste

or you know how low it must be
to be nearly done.

The mittens & potholders
reach for the handles and turn
the tray to the side for a better grip,
quickly, for the flame-tips rise
through slits in the stove top
singe-ing the hair on the wrist
'tween glove & sleeve,

The steam so fierce it sears the eyes
so I close them, turning slowly
determined not to slosh syrup

onto the floor, or worse,
and walk four steps in blindness to
a table in back
where I tilt the tray so the syrup pours out
of a corner down to a metal pot.

For a second I open my eyes to
sight in for the pour
and then the "spoawwt!"-sound
of sudden syrup on chilly steel.

I set the tray-pan back on the fire
then rush to pour fresh sap from
the can, before the tray doth burn.

I boil up another batch then pour it too in the pot
till it brims, and I carry it over the bridge
to the house, then bring back another pot

and on and on
till I quit at the dawn.

Back in the house
it's the peace of sap-sleep,
the smell of maple in moustache & hair
& reddened wrists from the sap sun.

The next morning Miriam & I
finish it off in the kitchen
half gallon by half gallon

heating it up to a boil
then checking the temperature.

We use a dial thermometer
clipped to the pan edge.
Sometimes the eyes get again
a hint of pain, leaning too close to read
the sugar-crusted dial.

Then one of us holds
a hammock-shaped padding
of cheese cloth hand to hand
while the other pours the syrup through it
into the jars to be sealed.

Some years the
sap keeps coming & coming & coming!
a never-ceasing flood to be boiled
till finally I yell, "No! No more!"
and pull the buckets from the trees
and pry off the spiles with a hammer's claw
& twig up the holes.

And then it's done for a year.

    Coda

There's nothing to it.
It's like the ocean
or raked Zen sand.

It's empty. Yet full
of the best.

It helps you to set
aside the fear
of bad luck & harm

to save all that was
and toss all that will
in the sweet roil of foam
in a tray on the hill.

—EDWARD SANDERS

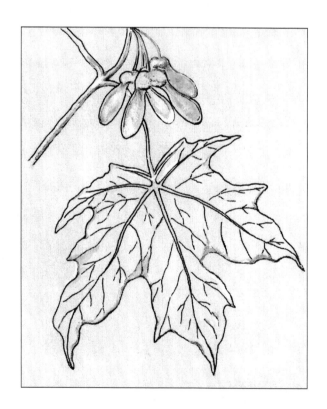

THE GALLANT CANADA GOOSE

Who has not paused, smiled, and searched the sky upon hearing the tumultuous cries of wild geese overhead! This sound has come to symbolize the changing of the seasons, longing, and wanderlust.

These magnificent birds, flying with necks outstretched, now form "Vs" across the autumn sky. They are often heard before they come into view, the leader calling to his flock, and it answering him.

The Canada Goose, *Branta canadensis*, is a large, handsome bird. It may attain a length of forty inches. The head and graceful long neck are midnight black; the shiny bill, eyes, legs, feet, and tail are black as well. The throat and cheeks are gleaming white. The body is covered with soft brown feathers above and gray beneath.

The Canada Goose is a native of North America. In the spring, it arrives to breed in the northern United States and Canada, and in the fall, it flies southward to spend the winter along the Gulf Coast and in Mexico.

Along their thousand mile journey, the geese descend to rest on secluded ponds and lakes. There, they eat the tender shoots of grasses and shore plants, small aquatic animals, insects, seeds, and corn. Sometimes a goose, too weary to continue in its migration, will join a flock of domestic geese. It is generally well received!

Canada Geese are quite adaptable in the choice of their nesting sites. Though they usually build the nest in tall grass or beneath low shrubs near the water, occasionally, they will build a nest on a cliff, or in a tree. They have even been known to take over the abandoned nest of an eagle or an osprey!

The nest is constructed of sticks, grass and moss, and lined with down and soft feathers plucked from the mother's breast. She lays about four or five creamy white eggs. As she broods them, the faithful gander stands by to protect her. He will grab an intruder with his bill, and beat it with his powerful wings.

When the bright-eyed goslings have broken out of their shells, and their fluffy yellow down has dried, they are ready to search for food, and follow their parents into the water. By fall, their plumage is sufficiently grown in so that they may accompany the adult birds on the long journey southward.

Geese are highly intelligent, exceedingly long-lived birds. It is known that they pair for life, and when one dies, its mate is often unconsolable, pining and refusing food. Occasionally, a pet goose will form such a bond with its human owner.

For this reason, the goose became a symbol to the ancient Greeks of loyalty and devotion. Burial markers of young women were carved with their images and those of their pet geese.

A SCARLET BLOOM
in the BARE WINTER BUSH

Many people have recently received Christmas cards depicting a male cardinal in a winter setting, the fiery color of its plumage contrasting beautifully with the sparkling white snow.

The bird's feathers are a brilliant red, except for those of the face and throat, which are jet black. Even the large, strong bill, adept at cracking seeds, is red. This bird is actually named after the cardinals of the Catholic Church, because they too are clothed in robes of scarlet. The female cardinal is a soft buff-brown, with a light red bill, crest, wings and tail.

We have few red birds, and of them, only the cardinal has a crest. It is of use to him in expressing his emotions. When he is calm, the crest lies flat, but any excitement causes him to raise it high. The female bird possesses a crest as well.

The song of the male cardinal is rich and clear, and reminiscent of that of the canary. Even the female bird sings a soft, sweet song. Both birds announce their presence with a sharp, distinctive call, "tsik".

The preferred habitat of the cardinal consists of clearings at the edge of woodlands, with bushes, young trees and vines present. Cardinals are beneficial birds, because they eat many weed seeds and injurious insects, such as beetles, grasshoppers, and flies. They enjoy eating wild grapes and berries, and corn, wheat, rye and oats. However, they never occur in sufficient numbers so as to be harmful to our crops.

The cardinal's nest is a deep cup woven of twigs, plant fibers, bark, and leaves, lined with rootlets and grass. It is concealed in dense shrubbery, vines, or low trees, rarely more than eight feet from the ground. Within the nest, there are three or four pale, greenish-white eggs marked with reddish-brown blotches.

While most birds form a monogamous bond for the duration of the breeding cycle, the cardinal pairs for life. The male cardinal is devoted to his mate, and is an excellent parent. He feeds the mother bird while she is on the nest; then feeds the babies, even after they have left the nest, and the mother is occupied with another clutch of eggs. The cardinal young have the subtle coloration of their mother.

Our familiar cardinal, *Cardinalis cardinalis*, ranges widely: from the Dakotas, southern Ontario, and Nova Scotia south to the Gulf Coast; and from southern Texas, Arizona, and southern California southward into Mexico.

One summer, my husband, Edward, and I visited his brother in Arizona. As the temperature soared to a record-breaking 120 degrees fahrenheit, we set out a shallow pan of cool water for the birds. When the first bird appeared, I was astonished to see a red cardinal! How strange and out of place it looked to me, in that harsh, brilliant light, the desert sand glittering and saguaro cacti all around us!

THE AMAZING OPOSSUM—
A LIVING FOSSIL

I f you are traveling down Glasco Turnpike, quite late at night, you are apt to see a droll creature, about the size of a cat, run rapidly across the road. Its long, shaggy fur has a silvery sheen in the moonlight, and its tail is naked and rat-like. When it turns to look at you, jet-black eyes stare from a ghostly white face. It is an opossum!

This ancient creature belongs to a family of very early mammals, the marsupials. The word marsupial comes from the Latin "marsupium" or pouch.

The mother opossum has a forward-opening pouch on the surface of her abdomen, like that of the kangaroo. The newborn babies, which are little more than embryos and smaller than bumblebees, must pull themselves, hand over hand, through the mother's fur to the safety of her pouch. There, each attaches itself to a nipple, where it remains for five or six weeks.

When the babies are sufficiently developed, they ride about on their mother's back, clinging to her fur with their strong little hands and feet.

Opossums can grasp well with their hind feet, because the first toe is long and flexible and opposes the other toes, just as the human thumb opposes the fingers. The hind foot of the opossum is like a little hand! (The first toe of the front foot is only a little opposable.)

The opossum has a wonderful tail. It is long, bare and scaly, and it is prehensile. When the animal climbs about in a tree, it can grasp branches with the tail to steady itself. It can even suspend itself by the tail for short periods of time!

The opossum is very adaptable in its choice of a home site. It may utilize an unoccupied burrow, a cavity in a tree or fallen log, a culvert, or an old squirrel's nest. It may even share a burrow with another animal, such as a skunk!

The opossum prefers to live in wooded areas with streams, but it thrives in farmland as well. In suburbs and towns, it may act as a scavenger.

The opossum's senses of smell and touch are good, but its vision is very poor. However, its sense of hearing is acute, which is of great use to it in detecting the movements of prey animals.

The opossum has a good digestive system and is quite omniverous. It eats small mammals, reptiles, amphibians, birds and eggs, and insects. It likes berries, apples and cherries, and most of all, persimmons!

Our opossum's ancestors came from areas that had tropical and subtropical climates. In order to survive in the North, the opossum must sleep through the coldest periods in its leaf-lined nest. Its metabolism slows, and it lives on the fat stored under its skin in the fall.

The opossum is a hardy little creature with great vitality. It recovers well from grave injuries that would kill other small mammals. When it is confronted by an enemy, the opossum may gape open its hissing mouth beyond ninety degrees, displaying fifty pointy teeth, and hold it open thus for fifteen minutes! As a last resort, the opossum will feign death. It will fall to the ground in a catatonic state. Lying on its side, with body limp, mouth partially open and tongue lolling out, to all appearances it is dead. Since many predators will not eat something that they themselves have not killed, they may just shake the opossum a few times, then move on.

We tend to anthropomorphize when judging the intelligence of other creatures. Opossums are shy, secretive, nocturnal beings, and the laboratory is not the best place to judge their abilities. We should not rush to dismiss them as slow and dim-witted. They are holding their own quite well in competition with "more advanced" mammals such as raccoons, foxes, dogs and cats.

They are expanding their range ever northward!

THE SMARTEST DOG *of* ALL

Many years ago, when I first moved to the country, I thought in my naiveté, "Surely I will soon see a fox!" After all, were there not daily encounters with raccoons, opossums, woodchucks, skunks, rabbits and such? The years went by, yet still no fox appeared.

As it turned out, all I'd had to do was convert an out building to a house for ducklings, and voilà, there was a fox. One day, my husband, Edward, called to me softly and pointed to the ducks' house. Creeping around the end, was a creature about the size of a small dog, with a very pointy nose and a lovely big, bushy tail. Its fur was a silvery grey. Everything in its demeanor spoke of a purposeful intelligence tempered with caution. As I watched the little fox investigate the door to the shed, I knew that from now on I would have to exercise great care in order to prevent the ducklings from becoming a feast for "Reynard."

The silver fox that visited us had demonstrated one of the several color phases of the red fox, *Vulpes fulva*. There is also a black phase, and a variety called "cross" with tawny fur, and a dark band across the shoulders and a dark band down the back, which form a cross. Normally, the red fox has golden-red fur with a white throat, and legs that are black on the outside and white on the inside. All varieties have a white tip on the beautiful bushy tail. All color phases may be present in one litter.

The preferred habitat of the red fox is a woodlands bordering old fields, with brush growing up that affords him cover for hunting. The fox's diet is very varied, the largest part consisting of meadow mice and cottontail rabbits. They also take domesticated poultry and ground-nesting gamebirds, their eggs, and fledglings. They eat insects, frogs, snakes and many fruits, and are especially fond of grapes. Although they will eat carrion, it is said they will never eat a bird of prey!

The fox may tunnel into a sandy bank to make his den, or locate it under a rock ledge, in a small cave, or even under the roots of a tree stump. The entry is usually concealed with vines and brush. If there is an abandoned woodchuck burrow handy, so much the better.

Foxes do not gather in packs, but go about solitary or in pairs. In the spring, when five to eight babies are born, the whole family lives in the den. Both parents care for the babies, and teach them to hunt. The family stays together until the following winter. When not raising young, adult foxes often prefer to sleep in the open, their wonderful tails wrapped around them for warmth.

The fox has a proportionately large brain, and is famous for his cunning. He has many clever ways to elude capture. When being chased, he may retrace his tracks, then jump to one side. He may run along the top of a fence or stone wall, run up a brook, or swim across a stream. He is good at avoiding traps. When placed in a situation where escape is impossible, the fox, as the wolf, may feign death. Perhaps the smartest thing he sometimes does is to make friends with the farmers' dogs!

THE WOODCHUCK—
A MASTER ENGINEER

Whenever I see a woodchuck, sitting up on his haunches at the entry to his burrow, I'm reminded of a chubby infant, dressed a furry snowsuit. I want to run over, grab him, and give him a hug! (Of course, if one did manage to seize a wild woodchuck, one would soon become acquainted with his big, sharp rodent incisors.) Still, every February 2, I'm envious when I see the zookeepers holding Punxsatawney Phil, on the television. Each year, Phil is roused from his winter torpor and hauled out of his burrow, so that, hopefully, he may predict an early spring. If he sees his shadow, however, the legend goes, there will be six more weeks of winter. This strange belief came from European settlers who used badgers, bears, or even hedgehogs in the old country to forecast the coming of spring.

The eastern woodchuck, *Marmota monax*, is one of the marmots, which are actually members of the squirrel family. It is about two feet in length, including the bushy tail, and has rather coarse, reddish-brown fur on the back and orangish fur on the stomach. It is a stocky creature, up to twelve pounds in weight; its legs are short, and the feet are dark. The woodchuck has large, white incisor teeth, unlike those of many rodents, which are orange!

The name, woodchuck, comes from the Algonquian word *wejack*. The creature is also known as a groundhog, or a whistle-pig, because of his habit of emitting a shrill whistle when he is alarmed. He will also chatter and grind his teeth when angry, and squeal and hiss when fighting with a rival during the mating season. Captive woodchucks, like guinea pigs, are known to purr when stroked.

Woodchucks normally inhabit the borders of woods, brushy fields, meadows, and pastures. They are even found along the edges of highways. Often, when riding in a car on the passenger's side, one can see woodchucks grazing on the shoulder of the road. Fortunately, they don't like to go too far from their burrows and rarely attempt to cross.

Woodchucks prefer to eat low, green vegetation such as, clover, grass, alfalfa, and dandelions. They are also quite fond of raspberries, blackberries, and wind-fall apples. They can climb trees, and will do so to avoid a predator or to obtain wild cherries. Only rarely, do they gnaw on bark.

When the woodchuck eats, it sits up on its haunches, holding its food in its paws and looking about for danger. If something frightens it, it whistles loudly, rushes to the entrance of its burrow, and dives in.

The woodchuck's burrow is an engineering marvel. The entrance hole, about a foot in width, narrows quickly within to about five or six inches in diameter; large enough for the woodchuck to enter, but not for a fox or coyote. The woodchuck loosens the dirt with its front feet, then pushes it backward and out with its hind feet. This causes a mound of dirt to accumulate at the entrance. This mound is useful as an observation platform on which to stand and look about for danger, or for sun-bathing.

The woodchuck digs inward three or four feet, then inclines upward for several more, then tunnels horizontally for fifteen to thirty feet. The upward incline usually prevents flooding. Off this main tunnel, there are at least two side chambers. One is for wastes; the other, lined with dried grass, is for sleeping, hibernating, and raising babies. There is always an escape tunnel with a concealed back exit. Abandoned woodchuck burrows provide homes for other small animals, such as rabbits, foxes, skunks, and opossums.

Woodchucks do not hoard food. They must eat heartily during the summer months, in order to store the fat they will live on during their long winter's sleep.

When it is ready to hibernate, usually in October, in New York, the woodchuck crawls into its nest chamber, and seals itself in with dirt. It curls up into a furry ball, the rates of breathing and pulse slow considerably, and the body cools. Occasionally it will wake up, take a few deep breaths to expand its lungs and eliminate toxins, then fall back into its torpid sleep.

Warmer weather awakens the woodchucks, sometime in March, and the male goes forth in search of a mate. Woodchuck babies are born naked, wrinkled, and only a few inches long. Their devoted mother changes the nesting materials frequently. When the babies are four weeks old, their eyes open, and the mother brings them their first green food. During the summer months, the babies make temporary homes near their mother's, then, in the fall, they establish territories of their own.

Sometimes, people move to rural areas, coddle bizarre, non-native plantings, and become enraged with the gentle, hungry wildlife that they have dispossessed. There are those who would wish to exterminate our woodchuck, the most benign of the squirrels. Let us hope they never succeed!

PLAINTIVE CRIES *in the* NIGHT

When returning home from a trip last week, at dawn, I heard the unmistakable call of a screech owl. Once this cry is heard it is never forgotten. The first time I ever heard a screech owl, it was, quite appropriately, one Halloween Eve. Off in the woods behind the house, an unearthly, quavering wail descended. Over and over the ghostly tremolo repeated. I stood transfixed. Finally, I realized that I was not hearing the cry of a soul in agony, but rather, that of an owl.

For all the impressive noise it makes, the screech owl is a small bird, only eight to ten inches in length, or, about the size of a robin. The females are slightly larger and heavier. There are two color phases—gray and reddish-brown. The feathers are also flecked and streaked with black and white, so that if the bird is seen in daylight, its mottled color will blend in with the bark of a tree. The screech owl is our only small owl with ear tufts.

Because he is a night hunter, the screech owl has developed remarkable eyesight. His huge, staring, round, yellow eyes are placed in the front of his head. The eyes are fixed in their sockets, so the owl must turn his whole head in order to keep an object within his field of vision. He can turn his head up to 270 degrees! The owl can also see quite well by day.

The flight of the screech owl is virtually noiseless and does not warn the prey. This is because the flight feathers have a velvety surface and soft fringes that cushion their beat on the air.

The screech owl has excellent hearing. The large, slit-shaped ear openings are covered with feathers that are attached to a flap of skin which can be moved forward, opening the ear. The ear openings are asymmetrically placed, which helps the owl locate the position of sounds. Furthermore, it is thought that the ruff of small stiff feathers surrounding the owl's face collects and focusses sound to the ears.

The screech owl's diet consists chiefly of rodents, insects and an occasional bird. He strikes the prey with his strong feet, and seizes it in his claws. His beak is hooked to tear into the flesh. The owl has an interesting way of eating; in the manner of a parrot, he holds his food in one foot and raises it to his beak, bending his head down a bit toward the foot. The owl eats the whole animal, then regurgitates the indigestible parts, such as feathers, bones, and hair. These rolled up wastes are known as "owl pellets." In late fall, the owl stashes slain mice in tree cavities for his later consumption.

The screech owl prefers to live in open woodlands, orchards, (especially old apple orchards) and suburban areas. It likes to occupy tree cavities, or even a nest box with an appropriate entrance hole. It will use the cavity not only for nesting, but also to retreat to from bad weather or enemies.

The owl often begins nesting while there is still snow on the ground. It lays its white, almost round eggs in the tree cavity with no nest lining. It is so protective of its nest, that it will strike unsuspecting humans on the head if they pass too close at night! (Sometimes people think they have been attacked by a bat.)

Screech owls mate for life, and are very devoted to their babies. They may actually sit together on the eggs!

The ancient Greeks associated the owl with the goddess of wisdom, Athena. Today, the owl itself has become a symbol of wisdom.

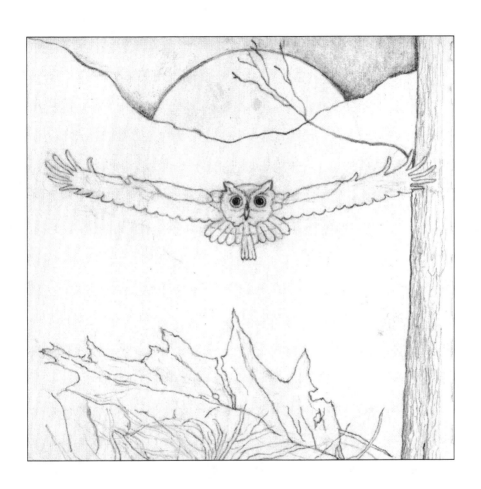

AN AMIABLE CREATURE
CLAD *in* ARMOR

The eastern box turtle, *Terrapene carolina*, can be found dwelling in moist woodlands, marshes, fields near water, and even, suburban back yards.

The most exciting thing about a box turtle is its wonderful shell. It is an excellent adaptation for defense against predators. The upper shell, called the carapace, is thick and domed, and attractively marked with yellow, orange or olive on a black or brown background. The turtle's ribs and backbone are actually fused to the carapace; the animal's internal organs lie beneath the shell.

The lower shell, called the plastron, has a hinge in both the front end and the rear. If danger looms, the turtle draws in its head, tail and feet, and pulls the plastron tightly closed against the carapace. If it is overturned by a predator, the turtle can easily right itself later.

Like other reptiles, box turtles have scales on their skin. The males have beautiful bright red eyes; the female's eyes are dark reddish or brown. Male turtles are usually smaller, but their tails are longer. Their plastrons are concave; the females' are flat.

Box turtles have an excellent sense of smell and touch, and can see well. Their hearing is not good, but they respond to vibrations. They like to simply shuffle along in the daylight hours, slowly and haphazardly, hoping to encounter something edible.

The most ancient turtle ancestors appeared two hundred million years ago, in the Triassic Period. Some had teeth, but no modern turtles do. They must tear their food with a sharp-edged beak.

The box turtle is thought by some authorities to be mostly carnivorous when young, and more herbivorous when adult. Actually, at all stages of life, they eat insects, earthworms, slugs, grubs, grasses, wild strawberries, and mushrooms.

I once purchased an adult box turtle from a pet store, having been seduced and confused by its charm. Today, I realize it had probably been plundered from the wild. The pet store owner assured me, erroneously, that the creature was totally vegetarian. I offered it all sorts of vegetable matter, but the turtle, Elizabeth, disdained to eat most of it.

It was early autumn and the house was chilly. Elizabeth, being cold-blooded like all reptiles, languished. I put her in an outdoor enclosure, but she still wasn't interested in her vegetables. Finally, a neighbor sent over her son with a jar of crawly, wiggly creatures found mostly under rocks. Elizabeth ate nine worms and grubs, nonstop. Yum-yum! She slurped up the worms in the manner of a child eating spaghetti. While no one noticed, Elizabeth, with renewed vigor, dug under her enclosure and returned to the wild. It was definitely for the best.

Since the weather was becoming colder, Elizabeth would soon have attempted to hibernate. In order to do this, a box turtle digs down about two feet into soil, or into a creek bank, or under rotting vegetation. It partially closes its shell, closes its eyes, and sleeps throughout the winter.

In hot weather, a box turtle may soak itself in shallow water, or bury itself in mud with just its head protruding. Its metabolism slows in a process called aestivation.

Box turtles are solitary except during the mating season. After mating, a mother turtle digs a hole in loose soil, places her round white eggs within, and covers them. She leaves them to be incubated by the warmth of the sun. After three months, the vulnerable babies, about the size of a quarter, must dig themselves out. It takes them five years to become adult, and four to eight inches in length.

Box turtles rarely range more than several hundred yards from where they were hatched, even though they may live for decades. In fact, they have been known to live over sixty years, and it is thought they may live to be one hundred!

RHAPSODY *in* BLUE

Last Thursday, March the seventh, I was kneeling on the sofa, gazing out of the living room window at a tangle of those wild rose bushes that grow now all over Woodstock. They (*Rosa multiflora*) were introduced decades ago. They are large, rambling bushes bearing tiny, pinkish-white, fragrant flowers once in spring-time. On a branch, in a steady snowfall, sat a male and female blue-bird! They were trying to eat the little wizened hips that still re-mained on a bush.

The eastern bluebird, *Sialia sialis*, is about six inches in length. The male's head, wings and tail are a brilliant sky blue, his throat and chest a warm, glowing, reddish-brown, and he is snowy white beneath. The female is a duller, greyish-blue above with a hint of red on her breast, and she is also white beneath. The blue color of the feathers is not a pigment color, but rather a refractionary color. It is best seen in favorable light conditions, when the bird is flying in the sunshine.

The bluebird possesses a sweet, melodious, warbling song that is softer and less complex than that of its relative, the robin. Its call is musical as well.

The eastern bluebird inhabits forest clearings, fields and pastures, the edge of woodlands, orchards, dooryards, and parks. He is the farmer's and gardener's friend, for he devours many harmful insect pests. He eats grasshoppers, flies, beetles and cutworms, and is espe-cially fond of caterpillars. He surveys the ground from his perch on a fence-post or a branch, then swoops down and pounces on his prey.

When insects are scarce, the bluebird eats wild fruits, especially the berries of the mistletoe, holly, and dogwood.

Early in the spring, the bluebirds build their nest in a natural tree hole, such as a hollow old apple tree or an abandoned woodpecker hole. A hole in a fence-post or a bluebird box is also acceptable.

The nest is a loose cup woven of grasses and plant stems, and lined with finer grass, feathers, and hair.

The mother bird incubates her pale blue eggs, usually four or five in number, for about two weeks. The father bird is affectionate towards her, and brings her food to the nest. When the babies become feathered, their lightly spotted breasts attest to the fact that, as is its cousin the robin, the bluebird is a member of the thrush family. Bluebirds usually raise a second brood of babies each summer.

In the fall, eastern bluebirds congregate in flocks of from less than two dozen birds up to those consisting of two hundred. Then, in a leisurely manner, they fly southward.

In the late 1800s, starlings and English sparrows were introduced into this country. With its gentle disposition, the bluebird is no match for these aggressive birds, which drive it away and usurp its nesting sites. By the 1900s, the bluebird population began to decline. The use of DDT on the insects that bluebirds ate also took its toll.

Today, the bluebird population is making a modest comeback due to the placing of suitable nestboxes by amateur conservationists.

At the end of a long, harsh winter, when we start to search in earnest for the first signs of spring, such as the emerging snowdrops, how delightful it is to see our returning bluebirds, and hear their lovely song once again.

A GENTLE REMINDER

Well into the 19th Century, the skies were periodically darkened by great flocks of migrating passenger pigeons. They existed in the millions. Their gregarious habits made them very vulnerable to predation by man, and they were ruthlessly slaughtered. They were shot, netted, trapped, and even clubbed down from the branches. By 1914, they were no more.

Our mourning dove looks almost exactly like a smaller version of the passenger pigeon, and was sometimes mistaken for it. It is about twelve inches in length, with a long, pointed tail. The head is rather small and the body plump, yet it is a more slender and graceful bird than our common domesticated pigeon.

Mourning doves are monomorphic, that is, the male and female are alike in appearance. Their plumage is a beautiful, soft, light brown, with glints of pink and blue. There are black patches on the shoulders and on either side of the head. The tail has a white border that shows conspicuously as the bird rises into flight, the wings making a loud "whistling" sound.

Mourning doves range throughout southern Canada and the United States, wintering south of the parallel of southern Connecticut. They inhabit open woods, orchards, farms, prairies, parks, and suburban areas with many shrubs and trees. They prefer to eat on the ground, although they will visit feeders in the winter. Since their diet consists primarily of seeds, small flocks of mourning doves fly after harvesting crews in the grain fields, in the manner of Biblical gleaners. They eat wheat, corn, peas, buckwheat and beans, and enjoy wild berries, and grass and weed seeds as well. When they wish to drink, they immerse their bills and are able to suck up water. They don't need to raise their heads for it to run down their throats!

The mourning dove is named for its drawn out, melancholy call heard most often in the spring—"coo-ah, coo, coo, coo." This is the time for courting. The male follows the female about as she feeds on the ground, his neck feathers fluffed out and his tail spread.

The mourning dove's nest is usually located in a pine tree or a brushy thicket. The female bird is the builder of the nest, and the male brings her materials. The nest is such a loosely constructed affair of twigs, stems, and straw that the one or two white eggs seem to be in danger of rolling out!

Both parents incubate the eggs and care for the young. The newly hatched babies are helpless, and covered with sparse yellow down. From their first day of hatching, the babies are fed with a remarkable, nutritious substance known as "pigeon milk." The parents both secrete it from special cells in the lining of their crops. This substance is rich in proteins and fats. In order to eat, the babies insert their bills into the parents' mouths, and the parents pump the milk from their crops into the babies' stomachs. As the babies get older, grain which has been partially digested in the parents' stomachs is mixed with this milk. It is thought that the number of birds that can be raised in each clutch is limited to only one or two because of this special method of feeding the young.

In some areas of our country, the mourning dove is protected, but in other areas, especially in the South, it is shot as a game bird. It is ironic that it is considered by some to be great sport to slay a dove, the very symbol of gentleness, devotion and peace.

AN ANCIENT FRIEND

Mallards are the most important ducks in the world, economically speaking, for they are the progenitors of nearly all common barnyard ducks. It is easy to habituate them to a pond with the offer of food. This quality, along with their friendly sociability, enabled them to be domesticated by the Chinese over a thousand years ago. They have provided eggs, meat, and feathers ever since.

The mallard, *Anas platyrhynchos*, is a large marsh-dwelling duck, with strong sexual dimorphism. The male is about two feet in length and the female somewhat smaller.

The mother duck's feathers, subtly mottled buff and brown, provide excellent camouflage at the nest. The drake in his breeding season plumage is resplendent. His head and neck are an iridescent green, set off by a white ring at the base of the throat. His breast feathers are chestnut-brown, and his body is a soft grayish color. When it is not the breeding season, the drake enters the "eclipse moult" and his feathers closely resemble those of the duck.

A good field marker for mallards, both duck and drake, is the metallic, purplish-blue patch on their wings, bordered with white and black.

The mallard drake's quack is soft, but the duck's is loud and emphatic. This characteristic persists in their domesticated descendents, and is one way of telling an all-white barnyard drake from an all-white duck.

How comical it is to watch mallards feeding in the shallows! They "tip up," that is, they practically stand on their heads in the water, curly tails and webbed feet waving in the air. They are able to locate food easily by means of their excellent underwater vision and sensitive probing bills. Mallards are primarily vegetarian, dining on pond weeds, herbs, grasses and grains. However, they will eat insects and other small animals during the breeding season. They prefer to sleep most of the day on calm water, then at dusk, ascend in a vertical leap and fly swiftly to small streams, ponds, and harvested fields in search of food. They return at dawn. A nesting mother, however, seeks food in shallow water nearby.

The nest is usually built on the ground—hidden among reeds, or placed on a brush heap near the water. It is constructed of grasses, rootlets and leaves, and lined with down plucked from the mother's own breast. She alone incubates the eggs and cares for the young. Whenever she must leave the nest in search of food, she covers it with grass and down.

The pale olive-colored eggs are eight to fourteen in number. Although only one is laid each day, they hatch within a few hours of one another, so that the mother can lead the ducklings to water all at one time.

The ducklings are covered with fuzzy down—yellow and smoky gray. They are able to leave the nest and follow their mother as soon as they are dry. They can swim and even dive before they are an hour old! Sometimes, people enjoying the charming sight of a mother mallard swimming across a pond, babies following her in a row one behind the other, are dismayed to see that one baby has suddenly disappeared. Unfortunately for the duckling, it has been seized by a snapping turtle, pulled beneath the surface of the water, drowned, and devoured.

In the breeding season, mallards are found from Alaska to northern Mexico. They winter south to Central America and the West Indies. They also inhabit most of Eurasia and northwest Africa. Great flocks of migrating mallards, flying at sixty miles per hour, are the very embodiment of wild freedom. Their domesticated descendants, enslaved to man for a thousand years, can not even fly a few feet to save themselves from predators!

The draining of swamps and "prairie pot-holes" (small ponds in the Midwest) for farming has had a detrimental effect on the number of mallards, but, happily, they are still abundant in North America.

THE HUMBLE-BEE

Is there anything that brings to mind more clearly a warm summer's day, than the droning buzz of bumblebees busy amidst the red clover flowers?

The bumblebees we are seeing now, in May, are all queens. They alone have survived the harsh winter; their families have perished.

Our queen bumblebee is large and beautiful, suitably regal in black and yellow velvet. She is one of the "social" insects. She will establish a colony with three castes. Her first offspring will be infertile daughters known as workers, then, at the end of the summer, she will produce male bees known as drones, and new queens.

Every bumblebee queen makes her nest in the ground, usually in the abandoned home of a mouse. It is already furnished with bits of lichen, moss, leaves and grass. The queen gathers pollen and nectar, and brings it to her nest. She makes it into a bean-sized ball, and lays tiny eggs upon it. When the eggs hatch into larvae, their meal awaits them!

The queen also makes a honey-pot of wax, about the size of a thimble, and fills it with honey. She places it just within the entrance to her nest. If the weather is cold or stormy, she will not have to go out and search for food.

After the larvae are full-grown, they spin a silken cocoon about themselves and pupate. The queen encloses them in waxen chambers. (Bumblebees secrete wax from special glands in their abdomens.)

After the young bees emerge from the cells, the cells are used to store honey. Because of its dual use, bumblebee comb is more irregular than honeybee comb, and the honey is rather rank.

The first bees to develop are small workers. They soon take over the gathering of pollen and nectar, freeing the queen simply to lay eggs. The hind legs of queen bees and workers have stiffened, upturned hairs which form "baskets" in which to carry pollen. The bee brushes pollen from her fur into these baskets.

The drones that appear in late summer have imperfectly developed pollen baskets and do no work. Their *raison d'etre* is to mate with the young queens.

A honeybee colony may contain one hundred thousand individuals; the bumblebee colony rarely contains more than five hundred. With the approach of winter, all members of the bumblebee colony die, with the exception of the young, impregnated queens. They will seek out a place to hibernate: under bark, in the ground, or perhaps, in a building. Torpid, they will sleep for the next six months. They will awaken in early spring, weak and lethargic but ready to seek out flowers and found a new generation.

Our bumblebee is able to defend herself with both bite and sting, but do not persecute her for she is our great friend. She is a most important pollinator of wildflowers and cultivated crops. In fact, she is the only bee that pollinates red clover, because the tongues of other bees are not long enough to reach the nectar!

In the 19th century, bumblebees were known as humble-bees. Emerson wrote, in a poem titled "The Humble-Bee":

> Wiser far than human seer
> Yellow-breeched philosopher!
> Seeing only what is fair,
> Sipping only what is sweet,
> Thou dost mock at fate and care,
> Leave the chaff, and take the wheat.

WILDCAT *of the* WOODS

A fierce predator stalks our woods and is only rarely seen. Secretive, wary, and elusive, it silently disappears when it senses the approach of man.

The beautiful fur of the bobcat affords it good camouflage. Its back is reddish-brown, mottled with indistinct dark spots, and its stomach is white with dark spots. Its ears have tiny tufts. A full-grown male normally weighs about thirty pounds and is three feet in length. The "bobbed" tail for which the animal is named is six inches long. The tail has several black bars, and its tip is black above and white beneath.

It used to be said of a man to describe his physical prowess, "He can whip his weight in wildcats." The bobcat is ferocious when cornered or attacked—hissing, spitting, screaming and growling. It can beat the average dog in a fight by lying on its back and raking the dog's eyes with needle-sharp claws.

The bobcat hunts primarily at night, by sight as well as scent. Its pupils enlarge dramatically in the dark, and its eyes have "reflectors" that catch any light that isn't initially absorbed by the retinas.

The bobcat can climb trees well, and often uses them for resting places or for refuge. It may leap down from a tree upon a hapless creature passing beneath. Bobcats usually hunt on the ground, slinking along, then rushing the last few yards and pouncing on their prey.

Bobcats are quite opportunistic in their diet, and, besides their favorite prey—rabbits and small rodents such as squirrels, mice, and chipmunks—they will take: porcupines, muskrats, beavers, ground-nesting birds, fish, deer, sheep and even calves. (A twenty pound bobcat can actually kill a two hundred pound deer, by leaping on it and severing the jugular vein with its teeth.) Perhaps, we are lucky that they avoid man!

The bobcat is not a noisy creature except during the mating season. Then, it issues forth the most horrendous screams, that are often mistaken for those of a hysterical woman! The mating season is in late winter, and the babies are born two months later, in April or May. The den may be under a rock ledge overhang, in a hollow tree, or well hidden in dense underbrush. There are between one and four kittens in a litter. They are born covered with spotted fur, weigh about one-half pound, and their eyes are closed. The eyes open in ten days. The babies are nursed for about two months, then their mother begins to bring them meat. Soon, the babies are ready to go on nocturnal hunting expeditions with their mother. The mother bobcat's tail is white on the underside of the tip. She holds it aloft, and the babies follow this "flag" as they hunt with her in the night. By fall, the babies may weigh twelve pounds. The bobcat family stays together for a year.

The bobcat, which is found across the United States and into Southern Canada, has actually increased its range since Colonial times. That is because it prefers to inhabit woodlands with clearings, brushy thickets, and even farmlands. These habitats provide more small animal prey to the bobcat than do virgin woodlands.

On May 1, 1996, in a yard on Abbey Road, Woodstock, a bobcat was photographed lying on its prey, a yearling deer!

THE MISUNDERSTOOD MOLE—
A WARRIOR *in* BLACK VELVET

Moles are small, plump, cylindrical creatures that live in underground tunnels they dig with their broad, shovel-shaped feet. Their bodies are covered with dense, soft, erect, velvety fur. This lovely fur can be rubbed in any direction without resistance, enabling moles to move quickly, forward or backward, through their tunnels.

Although the mole's eyes are greatly reduced, it can navigate the tunnels without bumping into walls, because of its exceedingly sensitive nose and sensory, hair-like structures that cover its face, back of front feet and tail.

In our area there are three species of mole: the eastern mole, the hairy-tailed mole, and the star-nosed mole. The star-nosed mole is quite odd in appearance, with twenty-two fleshy tentacles fringing its nose that help it sense its prey.

How many times have you heard someone say, "The moles ate all my bulbs?" In reality, moles are insectivores. They have not the slightest interest in vegetable matter of any sort. It is true, however, that moles may dislodge plant roots, and bulb-snatching rodents may utilize their shallow summer tunnels. On the other hand, moles stir and aerate the soil.

(Gardeners can protect bulbs at planting time by enclosing them in hardware cloth or pieces of the mesh sacks that onions are sold in.)

The mole is a fierce warrior, voraciously consuming enormous numbers of invertebrates. It may eat its own weight in prey in a day, and if deprived of food can starve to death in twelve hours. Besides eating earthworms, it devours the harmful larvae of insects such as lawn grubs, beetles, snails, slugs and millipedes. For garden pest control, tolerate the mole!

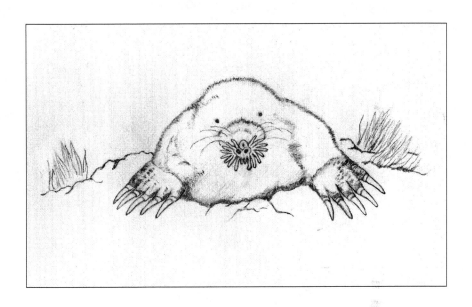

A CRIMSON HUNTER
in the WET GREEN GRASS

After a summer thunderstorm, when every surface still gleams and drips, our little red eft ventures forth. This diminutive creature, merely three inches long, is exceedingly beautiful. Its color is the red of paprika; each of its sides bears a row of vermilion spots encircled with black, and smaller black speckles.

The red eft is the juvenile, terrestrial form of a type of salamander known as the Eastern, or Red-spotted Newt.

The eft is an eager hunter, its black eyes rimmed with gold ever searching for insects and worms. When the prey is sighted, the eft quietly approaches, stretches out its neck, and, suddenly, shoots out its long, sticky tongue. The prey is seized!

The gaudy, salmon-red color of the eft is a warning to predators. The tiny creature's skin glands contain toxins. If something attempts to eat one eft, it will not try another! The skin of the red eft is rather dry, like that of the toad, and unlike that of many other salamanders who do not have lungs and must "breathe" through their smooth, moist skin.

The red eft may wander about the forest floor for up to nine years. When it is ready to mature, it seeks out a pond in which to spend its adult life and produce young. Now, the eft undergoes an amazing transformation. Its skin color changes to green above and beige below, but it keeps its attractive red spots and black speckles. The tail widens and develops a ruffled keel, useful for swimming. The adult newt eats small aquatic creatures in the shallow water.

In early spring, a mother newt lays 200 to 400 eggs, placed singly upon the submerged stems and leaves of water plants. They are translucent, with a little yellow yolk visible within. When the babies hatch out, they are legless with a large head and long tail. Just behind the head, on either side, there are three, feathery bunches of red gills. By late summer, the babies have developed lungs and their bright red coloration. They are ready to go forth and live on the land.

In this manner, the Eastern Newt is able to colonize new ponds, dispersing its species and continuing the fascinating life-cycle of its kind.

Many a jewelry designer, especially in the Art Nouveau period, has created a sparkling brooch in the sinuous shape of our graceful salamander.

A STRIPED BEGUILER

What an engaging little creature the chipmunk is, and how easily tamed! That is, how quickly he can train us to provide him with nuts and seeds! His Latin name, *Tamias striatus*, means the striped steward; a steward, in this case, being one who lays in provisions.

Chipmunks can stow away an astonishing amount of food in their inner cheek pouches. They look so comical with their cheeks puffed out, that people will feed them more and more, to see how much they can fit into their mouths. In fact, the noted naturalist, John Burroughs, meaning to "observe" the little creature, over a period of three days, gave a chipmunk five quarts of hickory nuts, two quarts of chestnuts, and much shelled corn!

This diminutive member of the squirrel family, nine inches long from head to tail tip, weighs only three ounces. He has chestnut-red fur, beautifully marked with five dark brown and buff stripes on his back and sides. He is white beneath. His large, shiny black eyes are also bordered with stripes. This coloration provides excellent camouflage amidst the leaf litter of the forest floor. The chipmunk has a flat, furry tail that he holds straight up as he runs.

Although the chipmunk can climb trees well enough, it prefers to scamper rapidly about on the ground. It is nervous and energetic, and chatters to its fellows with a variety of calls: "chips," "chucks," whistles and trills.

The chipmunk is fairly omnivorous. It primarily eats nuts, such as, acorns, pine nuts, hazelnuts, hickory nuts and beechnuts, and seeds and grains of all kinds. It particularly enjoys eating strawberries, blueberries, elderberries and raspberries, and wild cherries as well. It looks very cute to the human beholder, sitting up on its haunches, and clutching its nut in both hands, with its tail curved over its back.

The chipmunk may steal some flower bulbs, although his tiny cousins, the white-footed mouse and the pine vole, are the greater transgressors. The velvety little mole, no relative at all, is often blamed for these depredations. (He, of course, never eats bulbs, although his tunnels may provide access to the flower beds.) The chipmunk also aids the gardener, for it eats many injurious insects, snails, and slugs. There is a darker side to our little sprite; it has been known to seize birds' eggs, and even fledglings. However, these depredations are minor.

The chipmunk's preferred habitat is the edge of woodlands. He enjoys running about on old stone walls and perching on woodpiles. He will often site his burrow near a rock pile, or an old tree or stump. (Old root systems afford him many useful crevices.) The entrance to the burrow is a round hole about two inches in diameter. The shaft plunges straight down about seven inches, then veers, sloping downward two or three feet, to various chambers. Different chambers serve different purposes. Some are for the storage of food, the deepest chamber is the toilet, and the largest chamber, toward the rear of the main shaft, is for the bedroom. This is an oval room, about one foot wide and one foot high. Here, the chipmunk makes a warm bed of shredded leaves and grasses. His bed lies directly on top of a large heap of nuts and seeds. When the chipmunk wakes hungry in the winter, he need only reach beneath him for breakfast in bed!

The chipmunk moves the excavated soil several yards from the main entrance so as not to attract predators. Often, the clever little engineer digs a new entrance from below and fills in the original one.

Sometime in November, the chipmunk rolls up in a ball with his head tucked between his back legs, and his tail placed over his back and head like a blanket. His metabolism slows and he becomes torpid. However, since he isn't able to put on enough fat to get through the winter without eating, in the manner of a woodchuck, he wakes up from time to time. He eats some of his stored food, visits his toilet chamber, scampers about his burrow, and may even, if the day is warm, come out very briefly. Then, he goes back to sleep and becomes torpid once again.

Generally, at the time that the robins arrive, the chipmunks are ready to wake up and emerge. The male then searches for a mate. If a female chipmunk accepts him, (by no means a sure thing), after thirty days, three to five babies will be born. The babies are tiny, naked, pink creatures—helpless, blind and deaf. When two weeks old, they have faintly striped fuzzy fur, and can stand up. At three weeks, they can hear, and at four weeks, they can see. They stay with their mother for three and a half months, then, they are fully developed and ready to go forth on their own.

What a pleasure it is, after a cruel winter, to have the presence of these charming woodland creatures in the dooryard once again!

ENDLESS TOIL *for the* GOOD *of* ALL

The honeybee is a perfect socialist. It lives in large colonies that are organized into castes to benefit the whole society. The members of these castes—queen, worker females, and drones are adapted physically for their special role in the community.

Honeybees are insects of the Order Hymenoptera, those with membrane-like wings. They are fuzzy creatures, reddish-brown and black, with yellow rings around their abdomens. Their heads bear two antennae, large, compound eyes, one on either side, and three simple eyes between them. Honeybee eyes can perceive ultra-violet light! On their thoraxes are two pairs of translucent wings above, and, as with all insects, six legs beneath.

Honeybee colonies may contain up to a hundred thousand individuals! There is but one queen, several hundred drones, and the rest are all workers.

Worker bees, the smallest honeybees, are infertile females. Workers are equipped with tongues shaped like long tubes that enable them to suck the nectar from flowers. (Nectar is a sweet liquid produced by flowers to lure insects to visit them, and in so doing, carry pollen from one flower to another. This "pollination" helps seeds and fruits to form.)

The nectar is carried in special "honey stomachs" to the hive, where it is passed to other worker bees that add enzymes as they transfer it to wax storage chambers. The enzymes turn the nectar to honey. Worker bees' hind legs have "pollen baskets." These are long cavities in which pollen is packed to be brought back to the hive. On the lower side of their abdomens, there are glands that secrete wax. The bees chew this wax and form it into combs with hexagonal chambers for the storage of honey or the placement of eggs.

The tasks workers perform are determined by their age. First, they are nurses and feed the larvae. They also groom and feed the queen and build the waxen comb. Next, they become ventilators who fan their wings and set up currents in the nest to reduce the temperature and to evaporate and thicken the honey. Then, they become scavengers and cleaners. Finally, they go forth as foragers to find the flowers and collect the pollen and nectar.

Foraging workers perform a dance at the hive that imparts the scent of visited flowers, thus encouraging other bees to exploit the same food source. By the means of dances within the hive or just outside it, they can communicate information on the distance of the food source from the hive with great accuracy. They can also tell the other bees the direction from the hive of the food source in relation to the position of the sun. In some ways, the bee's sensory apparatus gives it knowledge of the environment which is closed to us except by the use of special instruments.

Worker bees also protect the hive by stinging intruders. Unfortunately, if a worker must use her sting, she gives up her life for the group. She cannot withdraw the stinger, and dies without it.

Those workers hatched in the spring work so hard that they die a natural death during the summer. Those hatched in the fall overwinter, and are able to labor for six weeks or more in the crucial spring months.

Drone bees, fertile males, are larger than workers. Their tongues are not long enough to reach the nectar in flowers. They have no "baskets" in which to carry pollen back to the hive. They have no sting with which to fight off intruders. Usually, only one will mate with the queen; the rest are utterly useless. As long as there is plenty of honey being produced they are tolerated, but, after the honey harvest is over, they are all driven from the nest and starve to death. The queen and her workers then dine on the stored honey throughout the winter.

Honeybee babies are little, white, legless grubs. They are all fed royal jelly (a nourishing secretion produced by nurse workers) for three days. After that, those designated to become workers will be fed "bee-bread," a mixture of honey and pollen, and those chosen to become queens will continue to receive the royal jelly.

The workers seal the babies into their waxen chambers, where they spin silken cocoons about themselves and pupate. The old queen then departs with a great swarm of bees to found a new colony.

When the first young queen emerges, she searches out the other queen cells and kills the developing queens within. After her nuptial flight, she settles down to the production of eggs, which she places singly in prepared chambers. A queen bee may live five years. She may lay two thousand eggs a day!

Honey has been the universal sweetener for thousands of years. The earliest record of keeping bees in hives was found in the sun temple erected ca. 2,400 B.C.E. by Ne-User-Re at Sakhara near Cairo, Egypt. As of 1991, the world production of honey stood at about a million tons a year; the main producers being the then USSR, China, the United States, Mexico and Argentina.

Today, a great calamity has befallen the honeybees. They are being parasitized and killed worldwide by two species of mite (one species inhabits the bee's esophagus and drinks its "blood!") There has been a tremendous die-off of bees. The bees in the Northeast U.S. were already stressed by an endless winter and the cavalier use of pesticides and herbicides in gardens and along the roadsides.

Don't think of the wildflowers as "weeds," but tolerate the goldenrod, asters, ox-eyed daisies, and black-eyed susans amidst your cultivated flowers. They all provide nectar to feed our bees.

Remember, without our bees to pollinate, most flowering plants would soon die out!

WILD CANARY *of the* WAYSIDE

I n his summer dress clothes, the male goldfinch is quite beautiful to behold, much like a tiny golden-yellow canary with a black cap pulled down low over his forehead, and black wings with white bars. His mate is much more subtly colored, with a brownish, olive-yellow head and back, yellow-white underparts, a black tail, and white-barred black wings.

Goldfinches are often called "wild canaries," not only because of their appearance, but also, due to their sweet, musical notes uttered when calling to one another in flight, or, when eating. At rest, they sing a warbling, tuneful, canary-like song. Goldfinches *are*, in fact, close relatives of the canary.

Goldfinches gather in exuberant flocks, flying in an undulating, wave-like manner, as though the tiny creatures were riding a roller-coaster and singing all the while!

Roadsides, brushy thickets, and weedy fields and meadows make fine habitat for Goldfinches. There, they can obtain the weed seeds, especially thistle, that are the mainstay of their diet, and grain, wild fruit, and the occasional aphid or caterpillar as well. (It is well known that goldfinches prefer thistle seed above all else. The French call the goldfinch "chardonaret," thistle in French being "chardon.")

Nesting does not take place until July, or even well into August, for that is when the thistledown is ready, and most weed seeds ripen. The female goldfinch builds a well-constructed nest, usually placed in a low shrub, a sapling, or berry canes, but occasionally, thirty feet high in a tree. The nest is a closely woven cup, fashioned of fine grasses, strips of bark, and moss. Sometimes, it is even decorated with bits of lichen. There is a thick, fluffy lining of thistledown within, to cushion the young.

While the mother broods her four to six bluish-white eggs, her attentive mate feeds her at the nest. Then, mother and father both feed the baby birds pre-digested seeds. Because nesting takes place so late in the season, there is but a single brood of young.

The male goldfinch dons his winter plumage in October. He becomes very similar in appearance to the female bird. His body is a soft olive-yellow, with bars on his wings, but with no black on his head.

Goldfinches are widespread in the Northeast. They are year-round residents, congregating in the winter in large cheerful flocks. Look carefully, and you may find among them their cousins, the pine siskins and redpolls, down from the too-cold north.

A MIRACULOUS MONARCH

The Monarch butterfly is one of the largest butterflies of America. It has a wingspan of four inches! The glowing, red-orange wings, decorated with white and veined in black, give the appearance of stained glass. The undersurfaces of the wings have a pale yellow ground color, so that the insect is hard to discern when it is at rest with the wings folded above its back.

The Monarch's head and body are black with white spots. On the head are antennae which end in club-like tips, and large, round, compound eyes. There is a wonderful coiled proboscis, or tube-like tongue, with which the Monarch sucks up nectar. The thorax has openings called spiracles, through which the creature breathes, and bears three pairs of legs and two pairs of membranous wings.

The wings are covered with tiny colored scales, that overlap in the manner of shingles on a roof. The Monarch butterfly, in fact, is a member of the insect order Lepidoptera, from the Greek word *lepidos*, meaning scale, and *ptera*, meaning wings.

The abdomen of the butterfly contains the digestive tract, reproductive organs, and more paired spiracles.

The Monarch butterfly is inedible, due to the toxic juice of the milkweed plants on which it dined as a caterpillar. Predators, in particular songbirds, have learned to recognize the wing patterns of toxic butterflies, and to avoid them. The tasty Viceroy, although belonging to a different sub-family of butterflies, looks remarkably like the Monarch. It is somewhat smaller, with a transverse black band on the hind wings. The Viceroy even mimics the Monarch's leisurely, smooth flight pattern. (Most butterflies, afraid of being snatched by a predator, exhibit a zig-zag flight pattern.)

The mother Monarch attaches her eggs, singly, to the underside of a milkweed leaf. The eggs are pale green and conical. Within three to five days, the ravenous caterpillars eat their way out!

The caterpillar has a head with a pair of small antennae, simple eyes, and strong jaws. Its thorax has three segments, each with a pair of short jointed legs with claws. On each side of the thorax is a spiracle. The abdomen has pairs of short fleshy "prolegs," a digestive tract, and more spiracles.

The full-grown Monarch caterpillar is gaily banded, with black, white and yellow stripes. It has two pairs of flexible, black filaments that it can wave wildly when excited, perhaps to confuse predators. If it is frightened, it may fall to the grass, where its stripes make it hard to be seen.

Monarch caterpillars feed on the blossoms and leaves of the milkweed. As they grow, they split and shed their skins. Eventually, they become about two inches in length.

When it is time to pupate, the caterpillar seeks a sheltered spot, such as beneath a window sill, a tree limb, or a fence rail, and there spins and attaches a dense silken mat. It takes hold of this fiber and splits open its skin once again. The caterpillar is transformed into an exquisite living jewel—the chrysalis. The Monarch chrysalis is jade-green, studded with golden drops. In time, it becomes transparent and the developing butterfly can be seen within. The chrysalis darkens, develops cracks, and the adult butterfly emerges. Its wings are soft, crumpled and damp. The butterfly pumps fluid through the veins, and the wings expand. When its wings are dry and have hardened, it flies off to feed on the nectar of flowers, and to find a mate.

(Butterflies are, next to bees, the most effective pollinators. Nectar is stored in flowers in such a way that insects wishing to reach it must come into contact with the flowers' reproductive organs. Pollen adheres to the insect, and is carried from flower to flower.)

In the fall, the Monarchs congregate in immense numbers. Spurred by hunger and cold, they fly southward by day. With strong wings beating rhythmically, they may attain a speed of twenty-five miles per hour. When they alight on trees which are already bare, their thousands of wings, appearing golden-brown in the distance, make the trees seem to be in full leaf!

Millions of Monarchs congregate in Mexico's Sierra Madre in special groves of evergreen trees. At nine thousand feet, the temperature hovers around the freezing mark and the butterflies are semi-dormant. Inactive, they don't burn up the reserve fat they need to make their northward flight.

In the spring, the Monarchs travel north in relays, the females laying eggs along the way. They reach New York State in early July. It is a mystery how the northernmost Monarchs, descendants of those which had traveled south, find their way to the ancient wintering places of their kind.

The Monarch is truly a wanderer. The Monarchs were originally New World butterflies; today, they have spread across the Atlantic to Western Europe, and across the Pacific to Hawaii, many South Sea islands, and even Australia!

AT THE EDGE *of a* PARKING LOT

Drive over the little bridge to the town parking lot on Rock City Road, and you will find at its borders a wonderful garden —full of color and burgeoning life. At the inner edge, pushing up through the very gravel, are sundrop primroses, whose pale yellow, cupped blooms contrast beautifully with the lavender-blue rays of chicory flowers. Pleasant field daisies and rosy, red clovers droning with bumblebees abound. There are tart-tasting sorrels, which look like shamrocks bearing little golden stars. Modest Herb Robert is present, with tiny pink-striped flowers and deeply-cut, ferny foliage.

Here is the ubiquitous prunella, its strange flower petals appearing at a distance to be fashioned from amethyst velvet. The wild snapdragon grows nearby, aptly named "butter and eggs" for its cheerful yellow and orange colors. Grasses gone to seed present a graceful counterpoint to the bright-hued flowers and the large rounded leaves of coltsfoot sprawled across the ground.

There is a stand of milkweeds, whose large fleshy leaves provide a fine meal for a gaily striped Monarch butterfly caterpillar. He shares the feast with several bristly black, white and orange creatures, the young of the milkweed tiger moth.

Farther back, there is the elegant Queen Anne's lace, whose dainty white flowers bend outward making of each plant a bouquet. The flowers that have already dried, curl in upon themselves, forming little "birds' nests."

Next, one encounters a drainage ditch. Here, are the splendid spires of gaudy purple loosestrife, rising over six feet high! It is flourishing amidst very robust cattails already bearing their fat, deep-brown catkins.

Dragonflies and damselflies dart about on gauzy wings, their bodies like burnished metal gleaming in the sunlight. Black swallowtail butterflies sip nectar from the huge flowerheads of tall Joe-Pye-weed; the flowers are the color of raspberry ice cream. Proud golden-rod lifts its plumes high behind masses of jewelweed, covered with spurred and speckle-throated, glowing, orange trumpets.

Between these flowers and the woods, there are tangles of the "multiflora" rose, now forming hips, elderberry shrubs with clusters of deep blue berries, and even viburnum, whose white flowers have given way to pendulous, glistening red fruit. Hidden in these bushes an impertinent catbird "meows" at the intruder. Wild grapevines festoon the saplings and Virginia creepers show their first brilliant red leaves—a portent of the fall display to come.

This is a garden that needs no pesticide, no fungicide, no fertilizer, no watering nor expensive fencing to keep out hungry creatures. What an excellent garden this is!

WATCHMAN *of the* WOODS

Our Eastern Crow, *Corvus brachyrhynchos*, belongs to the same family that includes the raven, the jays, the magpies, and the nutcrackers. (Nutcrackers are a type of bird that stores away nuts in the summer and fall and retrieves them in the winter.) The birds of the crow family, Corvidae, are believed by some scientists to be the most intelligent of all birds. They have performed even better than parrots on certain tests designed to gauge intelligence, and can actually understand the meaning of counting!

Crows are very versatile and adaptable, and although persecuted by man, they have thrived in his proximity. In the words of Thoreau, "What a perfectly New England sound is the voice of the crow... The bird sees the white man come and the Indian withdraw, but it withdraws not. Its untamed voice is still heard above the tinkling of the forge. It sees a race pass away, but it passes not away. It remains to remind us of aboriginal nature."

The voice of the crow is not solely a harsh "caw," but consists of many calls, including cackling, stuttering and even soft musical tones. It is thought that these vocalizations and their special meanings make up an actual crow language!

Our crow is a large, robust bird with a stocky build, about nineteen inches in length. Its long, strong wings make it a powerful flier, able to engage in aerial acrobatics. A crow on the ground walks about in a self-important manner that can best be described as "swaggering."

The crow appears to be totally black—the plumage, the eyes, the bill, and the legs. However, when one holds up a glossy, black crow's feather to the light, one sees that it has a beautiful green, blue, or purple iridescence.

The crow is omniverous. It is frequently killed by farmers due to its penchant for eating cultivated crops, such as corn and other grains. However, the crow also devours many injurious insects. It eats grasshoppers, cutworms, beetles, caterpillars, and grubs. It eats slugs, wild fruits, and even carrion. The crow kills destructive mice and other rodents as well. Sometimes, it raids birds' nests for eggs and fledglings, although it is often driven off successfully by the parent birds.

Crows are very gregarious, and have great collective intelligence. When feeding in a field, they post a sentinel high in a tree to warn the group at the first sign of danger. It is said that crows know the difference between a farmer carrying a shotgun and one carrying a harmless stick!

If a raccoon should appear, or an owl be discovered nearby, the whole group of crows would swoop at the intruder until it is driven from the vicinity.

In the winter, crows gather in great flocks to roost at dusk, preferably in an evergreen forest. These flocks may be made up of thousands of birds! By day, the crows go forth, often flying many miles in search of food.

The crow's nest, constructed by both parents, is a substantial creation. It is a large, bulky affair, fashioned of twigs, sticks, bark and vines, reinforced with turf and moss, and lined with grasses, rootlets, feathers, and hair. Within, there are three to five pale green or blue eggs, attractively marked with brown blotches and spots. As the mother crow sits on her eggs, the male bird brings her food. When the babies hatch, in April or May, both parents feed them— usually with insects. Long after the young crows have left the nest, they pursue their parents demanding to be fed. The family stays together for many months. Crows do not breed until their second year, which allows them to gain greater life experience before attempting to raise their young.

Crows make fascinating and long-lived pets, but they have some peculiar habits. They enjoy stealing small, bright objects, such as jewelry, and secreting them away. They also have the unfortunate practice of hiding bits of food in inaccessible places. Crows in captivity have been taught to speak words clearly, however, the cruel practice of splitting the birds' tongues has no effect on this ability.

The Eastern Crow is a year round resident in the Northern United States. Robert Frost wrote this of a chance encounter with a crow in winter:

A Favour

The way a crow
      Shook down on me
The dust of snow
      From a hemlock tree
Has given my heart
      A change of mood
And saved some part
      Of a day I had rued.

The Dying Crow

Dark wraith
Skittering up a dry creekbed
               wings outstretched

Were you looking for water
thirty feet ahead of you
            a shallow puddle remains
Seep at the base of a waterfall

You are too weak to get there
You crouch close to rocks at
          the edge of the bank
your cheek on a flat stone pillow
It's very hard to see you now

     Pass peacefully   Black Bird,

     Unmolested.

—Miriam Sanders
September 27, 2017

THERE ARE GIANTS *in our* HILLS

Five summers ago, Woodstock endured a severe drought. Creek beds were dry, and succulent green plants withered. All sorts of animals came down from the hills in search of water and food. Before then, bear sightings were infrequent, envied, and coveted.

One sultry afternoon, I looked out the kitchen window, and saw what I first took to be a large, black, Newfoundland dog in our back woods. I looked again, and saw that the creature was as long as the living room sofa! In fact, it was a black bear.

My husband, Edward, and I went out to photograph the visitor, who was snuffling about in the leaf litter beneath an oak, in search of acorns and small animals to eat. When it realized that it was being observed, it slowly shambled off in its peculiar, flat-footed manner.

Bears, like their close relatives the raccoons, are classified in the Order Carnivora, but are actually omnivorous, eating mostly vegetable matter. Besides acorns, beechnuts, and other nuts, they enjoy eating fruits such as apples, grapes, wild cherries, and many types of berries, especially blueberries. Bears are excellent tree climbers, and will climb trees and shake the branches vigorously to bring down the apples or nuts! Bears also eat insects, fish, birds' eggs and fledglings. They have even been known to take new-born fawns.

Bears have a "sweet-tooth," with a special weakness for honey. They open the hive, remove and eat the honeycomb, then eat the larvae as well. In early spring, when the bears emerge from their winter dens, they eat tender grasses and even strip the bark from conifers to get at the cambium and sap underneath.

Early summer is the mating time for the black bear. Bears can stand up on their hind legs and even take a few steps. They may stand up to wrestle with a rival or hug their mate! A pair of black bears will be affectionate to one another for about one month, then each goes its separate way.

In the summer, bears sleep in a shallow depression on the forest floor, or make what is known as a "bear nest." They break off tree branches and arrange them up in a tree, then sit or lie in them. When the serious cold and first snows of winter arrive, bears seek out a suitable shelter for their den. This may be in a cave, a crevice under a rock overhang, beneath a brush heap or the roots of a fallen tree. Sometimes, the bears excavate to enlarge the space.

Bears sleep through the winter, but not in the death-like manner of woodchucks. Bears are not true hibernators, because, even though their rate of heartbeat slows somewhat, and oxygen intake is reduced, their body temperature does not drop much. From time to time, they rise and move about. They are able to waken quickly and chase a would-be investigator out of the den!

While the mother lies dormant, one to three tiny cubs are born. They are blind, helpless and very hungry. The mother bear's milk is extremely rich and nutritious, and the babies grow quickly. (They weigh less than a pound at birth, four pounds when they emerge from the den in the spring, and forty pounds by the following autumn.) The cubs are very playful, curious and mischievous. They stay close to their mother, who teaches them which foods to eat, and to climb, swim and defend themselves. An adult bear usually has a slow, lumbering walk, but it can move very quickly to charge any animal it perceives as being a threat to the cubs.

Mother and cubs stay together the first summer, and den together the next winter. The following summer, the mother finds a new mate and the babies leave, or, if not, she may stay with them one more year. The American Black Bear, *Euarctos americanus*, may reach six feet in length, stand three and one half feet high at the shoulders, and weigh up to six hundred pounds. Its fur is dense, of a soft and even texture, and glossy. This fur had great commercial value in the 19th century.

The Native Americans revered the bear and never killed one without first apologizing to it. They chanted prayers deploring their need to kill the bear for food, warm clothing, and bedding.

Bears now appear regularly on the outskirts of town, and are frequent visitors to bird feeders. Bears are magnificent creatures but dangerous ones, and should not be encouraged to inhabit your yard! Bring in the bird feeders at night, or, put in just enough seed each day so that by evening they will be empty. Enclose and cover your compost, and never put in animal products. We, in Woodstock, are privileged to live close to Nature and her myriad creatures. We, too, should have respect for the giants in our hills.

A PLANTER *of* OAK FORESTS

The eastern blue jay, *Cyanocitta cristata*, is a passerine or perching bird, a member of the family that also includes magpies and crows. Members of this family are believed by many to be the most intelligent of all birds. They certainly have excellent memories!

The blue jay is a large, sleek, handsome bird with a prominent crest on his head. He is a brilliant sky-blue above and white beneath, and his wings and long tail are marked with pure white and black patches and stripes.

He is a bold and gregarious creature, and somewhat of a bully to smaller birds. He can be found inhabiting mixed forests of hardwoods, especially oak, and evergreens.

The blue jay's voice is often a noisy scream of "jay-jay," but he can also produce flute-like notes. He may shriek a warning if there is a predator such as an owl or hawk nearby; on the other hand, the blue jay himself can give an excellent imitation of the call of the red-shouldered hawk. He may utter this high-pitched call as he approaches a bird feeder, causing other birds to flee in terror.

Blue jays are omnivorous. They especially enjoy eating acorns and other nuts and seeds. Sometimes, they dig holes in the ground and hide the acorns within. Later in the season, they are able to retrieve them when needed. Those acorns that are not retrieved may grow into oak trees!

Blue jays also eat dragonflies and other large insects, and appreciate offerings of suet and peanut butter at feeders. Unfortunately, the blue jay has a predilection for the eggs and baby birds of smaller species. Fierce Nature balances this situation when the blue jay itself makes a fine meal for a hawk.

Blue jays usually site their nest in the fork of a tree, preferably a conifer. Both male and female birds build the nest. It is a bulky creation of twigs, bark, mosses and leaves, lined with rootlets. The mother bird lays four to six olive-green eggs, heavily spotted and blotched with brown. (They resemble miniature crows' eggs.) As the mother sits on her eggs, the male bird brings her her food. These normally noisy birds are very quiet in the vicinity of the nest. When the babies hatch, both parents feed them. It is amusing to see young blue jays, already almost indistinguishable from adults, still flying after their parents demanding food!

Yesterday, my husband, Edward, called my attention to a stump near the corner of our house. This stump, which had been present for over twenty years, was shimmering and glistening in the light, due to the wings of thousands of ants emerging from it for their nuptial flight. There were also many worker ants crawling about on its surface. This was an interesting but not really pleasing sight, only two feet from the house. Suddenly, a blue jay alighted on the stump, and began to seize ants and poke them under its wings, first on one side and then on the other!

This behavior is known as "anting." The ants' bodies contain formic acid, which is insecticidal. It is thought that this chemical, when anointing the feathers, discourages lice and mites on the bird. After the bird has performed this ritual, it bathes, oils and preens itself.

The range of our blue jay extends from southern Canada to the Gulf of Mexico, east of the Rockies. Blue jays are somewhat migratory. Although, in New York, we have blue jays year-round, the birds at our winter feeders may have actually migrated from colder northern lands!

THE RETURN *of the* RED ARMY

This is the time of year when some people are astonished to find their homes invaded by large numbers of ladybugs looking for a cozy place to wait out the winter. Normally, ladybugs hibernate beneath fallen branches or rocks. My friend Toby Heilbrunn, who lives in Bearsville, has just excitedly called to tell me that hundreds of ladybugs are assembling on the south and west sides of her house!

The appearance of the familiar ladybug, *Hippodamia convergens*, is often described as "cute." It is a tiny beetle, with a hemispherical body, and six little black legs attached to the flat side with which it can rapidly run. The shiny wing covers, which we see on its back, are red or orange, with thirteen black spots. The ladybug has a pair of long, dark wings folded crosswise beneath the wing covers that enable it to be a strong flier. If something molests a ladybug, it may fold its legs, drop, and feign death. After waiting several minutes, it will rise and quickly scamper away!

The ladybug especially enjoys eating aphids, mealybugs, scale insects, and their eggs as well. In the spring, the female ladybug lays her spindle-shaped eggs on plants infested with these insects. When the larvae hatch out, their dinner awaits them!

These larvae don't resemble their parents, round and shiny, but rather, are long and velvety black, with eight orange spots. As they grow, they shed their skins several times. Finally, they hang themselves up by their back ends to pupate. The pupae are somewhat rectangular, and black with red spots. After several days, the familiar adult ladybugs emerge. The adults also eat the same harmful insects.

The California citrus groves were once threatened with destruction by a pest called the "cottony cushion scale insect." Ladybugs were imported from Australia and introduced to the affected groves.

They ate and multiplied, and within several years the scale insects were exterminated and the trees saved.

Ladybugs, also known as ladybirds, were so admired in Medieval times that they were dedicated to the Virgin Mary; hence the "lady" in their name. The child's rhyme, "ladybird, ladybird, fly away home, your house is on fire, your children do roam," is thought to refer to the English custom of the burning of hop vines after the harvest.

Ladybugs are found in meadows, woods, and yards worldwide. In this country alone there are over 350 species!

A FURRY FORECASTER
of WINTER'S WEATHER

On warm days in the late fall, woolly bear caterpillars are often seen hurrying along, seeking out a secure place to curl up and hide through the cold, cruel months of winter. Such a suitable spot might be under a loose piece of bark or a fallen log.

The woolly bear is a handsome caterpillar, two inches in length. It has a shiny black head with two tiny yellow antennae, and is covered with bristly fur. This fur is black at each end of the creature, and reddish-brown in a band around its middle. If something attempts to seize a woolly bear, it curls up into a bristly and slippery ball, difficult to grasp. In fact, no bird molests it but the American cuckoo.

A woolly bear has six true legs, as do all insects. It also has eight prolegs and one prop-leg, which are mere extensions of the edges of its body, that help it to hold on to a leaf. There are tiny openings called "spiracles" along its sides, through which the woolly bear breathes!

The woolly bear spends the entire winter hibernating as a larva in its caterpillar form. Then, in April or May, it spins a silken cocoon about itself, incorporating loose hairs from its body which are easily shed at that time. The cocoon looks as though it were made of brown felt.

The moth that emerges is known as *Isia isabella*, the Isabella tiger moth. The tiger moths are named so because of their tawny, tiger-like colors. The attractive Isabella moth has a wingspread of two inches. Its pinkish-yellow forewings bear tiny black dots, and its paler orange hindwings, gray dots. There are six black dots down the center of its back, and six down either side as well.

The mother moth flies by night. She seeks a proper food plant for her young, and lays her eggs upon it. The larvae's favorite foods are wild plants: members of the plantain family, dandelions, clover and grasses. They rarely eat ornamentals or cultivated crops.

Since Colonial times, people have looked to the woolly bear to predict the severity of the coming winter. If the rusty-brown band of its fur is broad the winter should be mild, but, if narrow, the opposite!

MISCHIEF *in a* MASK

Our raccoon, also known as *Procyon lotor*, is a stocky, fur-bearing creature, up to thirty inches in length and thirty-five pounds in weight. His fur is thick and luxurious. It is usually brownish-gray in color, with lighter guard hairs, each tipped in black. This gives him a "grizzled" appearance. He is famous for his black bandit's mask bordered in white and his lovely bushy tail, ringed in black. (Unfortunately for the raccoon, in the days of Davy Crockett and Daniel Boone, woodsmen favored caps of 'coonskin with the tail dangling down behind.)

The raccoon is extremely intelligent, insatiably curious, and usually hungry. He possesses wonderfully dextrous fingers. These qualities may cause us trouble when he opens latches and enters poultry sheds and summer cottages. Many have awakened to find the garbage cans overturned, cleverly opened, and the contents strewn about for his inspection. Raccoons have even learned to open refrigerator doors!

One summer in the mid-1970s, long before the current rabies epidemic began, I would feed a young raccoon table scraps outside our screen door. Knowing that she had a sure source of food, she began to arrive earlier and earlier. One afternoon, I was demonstrating the "Lindy" (a dance of my youth) to my daughter. We were dancing and laughing, oblivious to everything else. When we finally paused to catch our breath, I noticed a determined tugging on my skirt. The little raccoon had arrived, noticed no food in her dish, opened the screen door and was trying to get my attention! Startled, I let out a small shriek. The dismayed and frightened raccoon began to run frantically about the house looking for an exit. By the time she had found her way out, the living room was in a shambles, with flower pots hurled to the floor. The little raccoon never entered the house again.

The raccoon is an excellent tree climber. When it walks, it is on the soles of the feet, like a bear or a person. In fact, its tracks look as though they were made by a human baby's hands and feet!

Although it is classified in the Order Carnivora, the raccoon is actually omnivorous. He enjoys eating wild grapes, peaches, berries, melons, and bird seeds at the feeder. He occasionally eats birds, their eggs, and fledglings as well. He eats small mammals such as mice and squirrels. He also eats crayfish, frogs, turtles and their eggs. When water is nearby, he will wash his food before eating it. In fact, the Europeans call the raccoon wash-bear. The raccoon has been known to rob beehives of their honey. His favorite treat is young corn, just before it should be harvested!

The raccoon is very opportunistic and manages to make a home in many habitats. It prefers to den in a hollow hardwood tree near water, however, it may occupy buildings, culverts, or even woodchuck burrows.

The raccoon is not a true hibernator, but it will stay in its den and sleep during the coldest spells of winter. In February, the male raccoon goes forth to seek a mate. If he finds a female who will accept him, he stays with her a week or two, but then she drives him away. Usually, four babies are born in April or May. They are helpless, only four inches long, thinly furred, with their eyes and ears closed. Their little masks are already present. After about three weeks their eyes open. When they are ten weeks old, they begin to follow their mother on her nightly foraging expeditions. They stay with her until the following spring.

Chubby baby raccoons, with their intelligent, shiny eyes, black bandit's masks and ringed tails are definitely appealing to humans. Unfortunately, they usually become too rambunctious as adults to be suitable pets.

A friend of mine, who lives in Greene County, New York, raised an orphan raccoon together with her own baby. They sat together at the table, and each received its own spoonful of baby food: first the baby, then the raccoon, then the baby, then the raccoon, etc.

When the raccoon reached adulthood, it was successfully returned to the wild, although it stayed in the general vicinity. It had been trained to ring a dinner bell outside the door and obtain a treat. For years afterward, the bell would occasionally ring and the raccoon would receive a doughnut!

Raccoons have many vocalizations. The babies whimper and cry when in distress, just like human babies, but purr when happy! The raccoon family members often quarrel, and it is alarming indeed to hear their angry shrieks, snarls and growls. The strangest sound the adults make is a descending tremulous wail. It is a plaintive, melancholy sound, much like that of the screech owl.

Edward once had a family of raccoons denning beneath the floor boards of his writing studio. He would complain that the loud afternoon snores of the snoozing raccoons were interfering with his ability to concentrate!

A GENTLE CREATURE FIERCELY ARMED

One winter's evening, when the cold was cruel and the sky crystal clear, Edward and I drove to the Magic Meadow for an unencumbered view of the stars, which sparkled like diamonds strewn by a cosmic jeweler upon infinite black velvet.

At the top of Meads Mountain, in the center of the road, we came upon a round and bristly object reminiscent in appearance of a western tumbleweed. The "tumbleweed" rose, ambled off into the woods, and slowly ascended a tree. It was a porcupine!

Bitter cold nights bother the porcupine little and it does not hibernate, though it will seek refuge in a den if the weather is stormy and wet. This den may be located beneath a rock ledge, in a hollow tree or log, or even in a derelict, falling-down shed. The porcupine usually goes its solitary way, but it will share an especially desirable denning place with others of its kind.

The porcupine is a large, nocturnal rodent, about three feet long and up to forty pounds in weight. It has a blunt face, with tiny black eyes almost hidden in fur. Its tail is short and muscular, and its legs are short and bowed. It waddles when it walks.

The porcupine is plantigrade, that is, it walks on the soles of its feet, as does a bear or a human. The porcupine's feet are furnished with long, strong claws, which help it to climb trees. The soles of the feet have pebbly bumps to keep it from slipping.

The porcupine's soft, woolly underfur is brownish-black. Amidst the many long guard hairs on its back and tail are thirty thousand needle-sharp, hollow, barbed quills. The quills are yellowish-white with black tips. They are actually formed of bristles of hair fused together.

If the porcupine is threatened, it would prefer to retreat and climb a tree, but if it is about to be attacked, it tucks its nose down between its front legs, arches its back and erects the quills, turns its rear toward the enemy, and at the crucial moment, slaps out with its tail. The quills are very loosely attached to the porcupine's skin, and when they hit the attacker's body they are driven in deeply. Body heat causes the barbs to expand, and every muscular contraction causes the quills to move deeper. The porcupine's underfur is shed in the summer, but the quills are always present in various stages of development (much as human hairs are on the head) so that the porcupine will never be left defenseless.

The porcupine has an acute sense of smell and touch, and it can hear certain sounds as well as a human. However, it is very near-sighted; it can't see well past several yards!

In the winter, the porcupine eats the tender inner bark of conifers, such as hemlock, pine and spruce, and of hardwoods, such as sugar maple, ash, birch and oak. A patch of bark the size of a sheet of typing paper is one day's portion of food.

In the spring, the porcupine enjoys eating the swelling buds of the sugar maple and the early raspberry leaves. As summer approaches, there are many herbaceous plants to be had, such as clover and dandelions, and berries as well. Even mushrooms are eaten. Sometimes orchards and cornfields are raided! The porcupine swims well, and his hollow spines make him buoyant. He will plunge into the water to dine on lily pads and watercress. Acorns and beechnuts are eaten in the fall. They have many calories, and are important food for animals preparing for winter.

The porcupine's passionate craving for salt is well known. He will gnaw almost anything humans have held. No handle of rake, axe or shovel left outdoors is safe. In fact, porcupines in winter have even resorted to munching on tires for the road salt on them!

The porcupine's breeding season is in the late fall to early winter. These normally silent animals then make all sorts of vocalizations: grunts, moans, whines, chatterings, barks.

After a gestation of about seven months, the solitary baby is born in the spring. It is born headfirst in a membraneous sac. Its quills are present but soft. (Thus, the mother is not injured when giving birth.)

The quills harden within a half hour and the tiny creature can defend itself. It is about one foot in length and one pound in weight. It is bigger than a baby bear! Baby porcupines are friendly and playful. When obtained quite young, they have made amiable, affectionate pets.

The fisher, a large weasel, is the porcupine's most dreaded enemy. It is able to flip the porcupine over onto its back and attack its underside, which is covered with bristly hair, but no protective spines. Man and his automobiles also take a toll.

Porcupines have an important place in the natural world. When porcupines strip off enough bark to kill trees, they create openings in the forest canopy. This allows sunlight to penetrate, and creates an environment conducive to a succession of varied species of plants and trees.

Porcupines clip off branches that are in their way when they wish to reach acorns and beechnuts. These branches fall to the ground and are an important food source for the deer in winter, when the snow is deep and browse is scarce.

Ottawa and Cree Native Americans utilized porcupine quills to decorate birch bark boxes, the Sioux to decorate moccasins, and the Crow to decorate buckskin shirts, elkskin robes and war bonnets.

It is a mistake to judge our lethargic porcupine as dull and witless. In the laboratory, he is adept at finding his way through mazes, his memory is quite good, and he is quicker than a monkey at extricating himself from a cage!

THE MYSTERIOUS MISTLETOE

This is the time of year when, should a young man notice a girl standing beneath a sprig of mistletoe hanging over a doorway, he would be permitted to steal a kiss. Some say, "One kiss for each berry on the plant!"

In ancient times, according to the Roman scholar and historian Pliny, the Druids revered the mistletoe. They held their sacred rites in oak groves, and whatever grew upon the oak, such as the mistletoe, was thought to be a divine gift. When a mistletoe plant was discovered, a priest, clad in a white robe, cut it off the branch with a golden knife. Two white bulls were then sacrificed on this spot. The mistletoe was thought to have magical properties and healing powers. It was taken in a drink as a cure for sterility and an antidote for poisons, curiously, since mistletoe itself may be fatally poisonous!

In Scandinavian mythology, Balder, the sun god, was slain by the blind god Hod, with a branch of mistletoe. Balder, son of Odin and the goddess Frigg, was radiantly beautiful and greatly loved. Frigg elicited a promise from every being and thing on earth, except the mistletoe, not to harm Balder. She had, unfortunately, deemed the mistletoe too young to take an oath!

The mistletoe is a partially parasitic plant. Although it has leathery, green leaves with chlorophyll that manufacture food in the presence of sunlight, it depends on a host plant to provide it with water and minerals. The mistletoe accomplishes this by utilizing small modified roots known as haustoria that penetrate the host.

The mistletoe has inconspicuous, yellowish flowers and plump, round, ripe berries whose pulp is transparent and viscous. The pulp is so sticky, in fact, that bird-lime (a substance smeared on branches to catch birds upon alighting) was sometimes made from it.

The mistletoe is parasitic on a wide variety of trees, both evergreen and deciduous. Among these are apple, poplar, willow, oak, maple and larch. Seed dispersal occurs in this manner: sticky seeds adhere to a bird's beak when it eats mistletoe berries. When it flies to another tree and wipes its beak on a branch to clean it, the seeds cling to the bark and are "planted". Mistletoe grows slowly and its life span is usually determined by that of the host plant.

In New Zealand, there are gigantic mistletoes that can grow to a height and width of nine feet and live for a century! At Christmas, they produce large, scarlet blooms, tightly closed. Only certain native birds can open the buds and pollinate the flowers, but their numbers are being decimated by non-native animals, such as rats, ferrets and cats. A native bee can also open the buds, but only the birds eat the fruit and disperse the seeds. Therefore, scientists are greatly concerned about the future of these interesting plants.

A DIMINUTIVE DESPOT

During the twenty years that we lived on a three acre property in Woodstock, we had the companionship of only one red squirrel. His fur was so startlingly red, and his manner so imperious that he had to be named "Eric the Red."

What self-righteous indignation pours forth from a red squirrel if a human or any other creature enters into what it has deemed its own territory. There is much vituperative chattering, and the angry stamping of little feet on a branch! We had a merry pack of gray squirrels all much larger than Eric, and if any of them dared to approach Eric's favorite hemlock tree, he would chase them in a fierce manner with obvious intent to nip!

The colonists in New England had a name for our feisty chatter-box—the Chickaree. He is also known as the pine squirrel, because of his great predilection for pine nuts. In fact, the red squirrel will assemble a hoard of pine cones, unhidden, several feet high and wide. He will sit upon it , extract the nuts from the cones, then throw down the inedible parts until there is a great mound of pine cones and detritus known as a "midden." He adds new, fresh cones to this heap yearly. The red squirrel's other caches of food are well hidden in stone walls, hollow trees, and crevices. A bushel of nuts may be stored in one tree alone!

In the winter, the red squirrel may make tunnels under the snow, from the base of his home tree to food cache to food cache. He may also nip off and eat the terminal buds of evergreen trees.

In the spring, the red squirrel enjoys a special treat. He scrapes out a tiny cavity with his sharp chisel teeth on a trunk or branch of a maple or birch tree, then eagerly laps up the sweet sap that accumulates there.

Summer's bounty brings a fine diet for the little squirrel. There are all sorts of buds, roots and berries to be had, and insects as well.

He will even eat carpenter ants found in woodpecker holes. A red squirrel is quite fond of mushrooms. It bites off pieces, tucks them up amongst tree twigs to dry, then stores them away for winter use!

In November, Eric's fur became brighter in hue. A black stripe along his side divided his glistening, red back fur from his grayish-white underparts. He even developed fancy little tufts on his ears! He had built a cozy nest in an old shed next to the hemlock tree. A red squirrel prefers to nest in a tree cavity, but if none is available, it is quite opportunistic. Sometimes, it makes an outside nest in a conifer or a tangle of grapevines. This creation is placed on a base of twigs, with an outer wall of leaves and a lining of soft mosses and grasses. It even has a tiny door to keep out the cold. Sometimes, the nest is made in an elaborate undergound burrow, with many chambers. It might even be made in your attic!

The nest is a snug home for the tiny squirrel babies, usually four in number, born naked and blind in the spring. They are only about four inches long, including their tails. Within ten days they are nicely furred. They are nursed for two months, then they start to make short forays from the nest. By fall, they are mature squirrels ready to set up housekeeping.

The red squirrel is diurnal, that is, active by day, but sometimes, especially if the moon is bright, the little insomniac comes out of his safe nest to indulge in a night-time snack. Unlucky is he if there is an owl, also hungry, nearby!

All winter, Eric ran about in the tree tops conducting his important squirrel business, and only disappeared on the coldest of days, presumably to sleep in his nest with his tail wrapped around him like a scarf.

One afternoon, I glanced out the kitchen window toward Eric's favorite hemlock tree. I was expecting the pleasant sight of Eric perched on a branch, enjoying a nut, his lovely tail curved over his back. Instead, I saw a huge, red-tailed hawk thrusting himself against the trunk of the tree. I realized that he was attempting to seize and pin down the squirrel! (This hawk had been about the property for days, dining on chipmunks and plump mourning doves.) I ran outside, yelling and flailing my arms to drive him away. I interfered with the work of Mother Nature, and Eric was saved that day.

AN INVASION *of* VOLES

One bitter-cold January night, Edward and I, in an attempt to amuse a houseguest, decided to take him to Fleischmanns to a "real country auction." Our teen-age daughter had seen enough auctions, and finding the company of the guest tedious, elected to stay home and do her homework in typical teenager fashion, in front of the television set. She had spread her papers on the floor around her easy chair. Noticing movement out of the corner of her eye, she was dismayed to see five small rodents circling her chair, and worse yet, seizing, pulling and tearing at one page of homework!

Tucking her legs up under her, she reached for the phone and called a girlfriend to complain that she was home alone being attacked by "rats!"

In the meantime, Edward, the houseguest and I were stranded in Fleischmanns due to a frozen car radiator. When we were finally able to return home, quite late, we were astonished to find vole visitors still wandering about the living room, and an indignant daughter brandishing a crumpled sheet of homework. The voles were small, stocky creatures, with reddish-brown fur above and silvery-grey beneath, quite different in appearance from our usual rodent companions—the white-footed mice.

Where the white-foot's black eyes are huge and protruding, the vole's are like tiny beads. The white-foot's nose is rather long; the vole's is short and blunt. The white-foot's ears are large; the vole's are small and almost hidden in its fur. The white-foot has a long furred tail that helps it keep its balance as it climbs and leaps about, but the ground-dwelling vole's tail is short and furred.

I grabbed a broom and attempted to sweep one of the voles out of the room. I was amazed to see the diminutive creature sit up on its haunches and snap and bite at the broom while squeaking with apparent rage. It fought the broom all the way to the outside door! A second vole, caught in a live trap, showed its displeasure as well, with squeaks, squeals and gnashing teeth. What feisty little creatures they were! The other three voles disappeared and were not seen again. Presumably, they entered their system of tunnels that lay beneath the snow, and made their way back to their burrows and cozy nests. (Voles' nests are rounded, ball-like affairs made of coarse grasses, weeds or leaves on the outside, and the softest, finest materials available on the inside.)

Voles normally lead lives of concealment. They create tunnels through meadow grasses or leaf litter on the forest floor in summer, and through the snow in winter. They inhabit elaborate burrow systems just beneath the surface of the ground. These systems are sometimes mistaken for those of a mole, which they resemble, even to the pile of excavated debris at the tunnel entrances.

Voles must stay hidden as much as possible because they are a most important food source for many carnivores. They are preyed upon by hawks, owls, snakes, bobcats, foxes, raccoons and their most terrifying enemies, who enter their very homes, the weasels.

To make up for this constant loss of life, voles are quite prolific. A mother vole may raise thirteen families in a year, each having six babies on the average, and these babies, born naked and helpless, are themselves ready to reproduce in less than one month!

These nervous little creatures are intelligent, with a keen sense of hearing and of smell. They have a wide field of vision. Their hearts beat rapidly and they breathe rapidly. They expend energy so quickly that they must consume a considerable amount of food to stay alive. Unfortunately, the food they eat may be the farmer's grain or root vegetables, the gardener's bulbs, or the bark at the bottom of the nursery man's apple trees. When the snow melts away in the spring, valuable trees are sometimes found to be completely girdled. Native Americans used to turn the tables on the voles, and dig into their burrows to locate the hoards of edible roots and grains stored within.

Voles do not ordinarily enter human dwellings, but, since we had already had a colony of little brown bats in the attic, red-backed salamanders in the bathroom, a flying squirrel in the kitchen, and countless merry mice careening through the cupboards, why not voles in the living room? Our woodland neighbors seem to think that our old house is a nice, warm, hollow tree!

THE COURAGEOUS CHICKADEE

How cheering it is on a gray winter day to be visited by a flock of chickadees accompanied by white-breasted nuthatches, tufted titmice, and downy woodpeckers. They seem so good-natured as they constantly call to one another, "chick-a-dee-dee-dee" while they make the rounds of all the neighborhood bird-feeders. They seize sunflower seeds and fly off to the bushes to open them by holding them down with their feet and hammering them with their strong little beaks. They also enjoy the offerings of suet.

Chickadees are tiny, plump members of the tit family, attired in shining black caps and bibs. Their cheeks are white, their backs are gray, and their dark gray wings and tail feathers are edged in white. Their grayish-white breast feathers change to a warm buff color on their sides.

Chickadees are so bold that they can easily be trained to take food from the hand. I was delighted the first time a chickadee stood on my open palm to accept a sunflower seed! In the words of Thoreau regarding his chickadees, "They were so familiar that at length one alighted on an armful of wood which I was carrying in and pecked at the sticks without fear." (Chickadees peck out the eggs of insects from the crevices of tree bark.)

In warm weather, chickadees eat many injurious insects such as leaf hoppers and the tent caterpillars that damage our fruit and shade trees. Later in the season, they eat wild berries and weed and tree seeds. As my husband, Edward, once wrote,

> The chickadee
> biting and shaking
> the cluster
> of maple seeds

like six tiny

mountain maracas

Chickadees are tiny woodland acrobats. It is amusing to see them clinging upside-down as they peck out the seeds of pine cones or the insect eggs from a twig. Farmers used to lure chickadees into their orchards by hanging up suet, so that the little birds would come and also find the eggs of harmful insects. One chickadee may destroy several hundred insect eggs in just one day!

In October and November, the chickadees may be observed seeking out holes to be used as night-time roosting places in the coming winter. Chickadees are among the hardiest of small birds. It is remarkable that such tiny creatures are able to maintain their body temperature of 106 degrees Fahrenheit when awake, and only two or three degrees less while they sleep through our winter nights! (Their insulating layers of feathers and subcutaneous fat help them to conserve heat, and they produce heat by metabolizing the food they eat, and when necessary, their own body fat.)

In February, the chickadees add a new musical call to their cheerful trills—a clear, haunting whistle of fee-bee, the latter note descending.

In March and April, the chickadees are often seen inspecting holes that might be suitable for nesting sites. If there are no old woodpecker holes handy, chickadees will use their tiny strong beaks to excavate cavities in the soft wood of rotting tree limbs or trunks. They may deposit nesting materials in several holes before making their final selection. The birds carry away the excavated wood chips from the chosen hole so that there will be no outward "evidence" of the nest's existence. The nest itself is a mass of moss, grass and plant down, softly lined with feathers, and perhaps, rabbit fur. The eggs are six to eight in number, white, and decorated with reddish-brown speckles. The mother and father birds take turns feeding the babies, sometimes in a relay: the mother may feed the babies, and as she is leaving the nest, the father bird approaches, passes her his beakful of insects, and in she goes again! It is a good idea to leave some old "snags" (dead trees) around the property for the use of our cavity-nesting birds, and for flying squirrels as well.

After Christmas, some people set out their Christmas trees festooned with treats for the chickadees such as pine cones dipped in fat, peanuts, and even doughnuts!

THE GIANT MOUSE

In the Town of Woodstock, on the Wittenberg Road just past the Odd Fellows Lodge, is a wonderful marshy pond created by beavers. Among the many happy creatures that live there is one that often goes unnoticed. In the shadow of his larger, more flamboyant relative, the beaver, the equally industrious muskrat conducts his affairs.

Imagine a giant mouse, two feet long, including his ten inch tail, and weighing four pounds! Such a creature is our muskrat, the largest of the New World mice and closely related to the vole.

He is a chunky, short-legged animal, better developed for life in the water than on land. He can't run fast but he is an excellent swimmer. In fact, his hind feet are actually webbed! His tail is long, sparsely haired, scaly and black. It is vertically compressed, that is, flattened from side to side. When a muskrat swims, the tail acts as a rudder. The muskrat has dark, chestnut-brown fur on his back, silvery-gray on his belly, and white on his throat. His underfur is soft, fine, dense and waterproof. He has an outer coat of coarse, glistening guard hairs.

With his rounded head, blunt face, shiny black eyes, small ears almost hidden in fur, and long whiskers about his nose and mouth, he looks quite like a huge meadow mouse!

Our talented muskrat has the engineering skills of the woodchuck and the beaver combined. If the bank bordering his pond or stream is suitable, he may excavate an elaborate burrow.

From an entrance beneath the surface of the water, he will dig a tunnel into the bank leading upward to a cozy leaf-lined chamber situated above the water line, but still several feet below ground level. Small subsidiary tunnels connect the burrow to the surface of the bank. These are ventilation shafts, and are loosely filled with vegetation. There may also be escape tunnels, whose entrances are camouflaged.

The muskrat builds a lodge for winter. To the observer, the lodge appears to be a hummock—a natural feature of the marsh and not a habitation at all. On a large platform of vegetation, he piles aquatic plants, such as cattails, phragmites, and sedges mixed with twigs, leaves and mud. When the dome-shaped mound is several feet high, he excavates it from within—hollowing it out until a chamber is formed. This chamber is softly lined with moss and leaves. A passage leads down to the water beneath and there is a hole for ventilation.

In winter, the muskrat dives down from the lodge's underwater opening, swims under the ice and forages for roots. He can stay under water twelve minutes. In an emergency, he may resort to eating his own house!

The muskrat leads as furtive and fear-drenched a life as that of its cousin, the meadow mouse. It builds feeding stations, which are little islands created of mud, twigs, and other vegetation, wedged between plant stalks. Here, the muskrat sits while eating, ready to dive into the comparative safety of the water at the first sign of an enemy. He also digs canals to connect his feeding areas so that he can remain in the water as much as possible.

The muskrat enjoys eating all sorts of aquatic plants such as bulrushes, sedges, arrowheads, reeds, and the roots of water lilies, but its favorite food of all is cattail. It eats the cattails' stems and roots and utilizes the stalks for lodge building as well. In fact, the muskrat eats so many water plants that it creates open water in marshy areas and provides habitat for migrating waterfowl.

Unlike the beaver, the muskrat is not solely a vegetarian. It will eat snails, clams, mussels and crawdads, and frogs, fish, turtles and insects.

Unfortunately for the muskrat, many creatures *find* him to be delicious. He is preyed upon by hawks, owls and snapping turtles. His babies are seized by large pickerels and pikes. His most serious enemies are members of the weasel clan, and of these, the worst is the mink, for it can follow him right into his home! Muskrats are sold to humans as food under the names "marsh rabbit" or, "marsh hare."

Muskrat males are fierce fighters amongst themselves. They are jealous householders who will defend their territories with much squealing, chasing and biting. This feistiness and courage comes in good stead when they must defend themselves against enemies. With gnashing incisors, a cornered muskrat will fight to the death.

Some say the name muskrat comes from the Algonquin word, "musquash," and some say it refers to the musk secreted by two special glands between the creature's hind legs. He uses this substance to mark his territory and to attract females in the breeding season.

Baby muskrats are born naked and blind. They are only about four inches long, and weigh less than an ounce. In just two weeks, they are so developed that they can begin to learn to swim! The mother alone is their teacher and protector. In six months, the babies are fully grown and independent. Fortunately, a mother muskrat can produce three litters a year, each having three to seven young. Only thus are muskrats able to maintain their numbers when millions are slain yearly by their natural enemies, hunters and trappers. The muskrat's fine fur is sold under deceptive names, such as, Hudson seal, Russian otter, red seal or river mink.

On March 2, 1997, the *Kingston Freeman* reported that 275 Fish and Game officers of the Department of Environmental Conservation are to receive new winter hats, cut of cloth with muskrat fur brims, at a cost to the State of $9,350. Because it isn't deemed cost-effective to raise muskrats in captivity, they are caught by cruel leg-hold traps. These traps cause the animals terrible suffering, and they will sometimes gnaw off their own feet in their desperation to escape. Surely, those hat brims could also be cut of cloth, and the innocent muskrats be spared!

RETURN *of the* REDWINGS

John Burroughs called red-winged blackbirds "red-shouldered starlings." This is what he wrote of them as harbingers of spring: "When the red-shouldered starlings begin to gurgle in the elms or golden willows along the marshes and water-courses, you will feel spring then; and if you look closely upon the ground beneath them, you will find that sturdy advance guard of our floral army, the skunk cabbage, thrusting his spear-point up through the ooze, and spring will again quicken your pulse."

Most red-winged blackbirds, also known as redwings, spend their winters south of the Ohio and Delaware Rivers, where they forage in large flocks amidst cowbirds, rusty blackbirds, grackles and starlings.

In March, male redwings return to Woodstock. In great smoky-black undulating clouds, they descend on the wetlands, eager to stake out and defend their territories. These are glossy, black birds with long tails, somewhat smaller than robins. They have beautifully contrasting scarlet shoulders edged with yellow, which they display with half-spread wings as they sing a melodious "o-ka-lee" in ascending notes. Soon the swamps resound with their musical calls.

About three weeks later, the female birds arrive. They are dusky brown, with breasts heavily streaked with brown, black and buff. They almost appear to be birds of another species!

After tumultuous courtships involving much chasing about the swamp, the males and females settle down to raise their families. Some males are monogamous and some polygamous. Those which have more than one family, like feathered Mormons of old, must defend them all!

The redwing nest is usually built in the month of May, by the mother bird alone. Since the redwings prefer a marshy, swampy habitat, or at least close proximity to a pond or slow moving creek, the nest is frequently concealed amongst bulrushes, reeds or cat-tails, or situated low in a bush such as a pussy willow. The nest is often placed just a few feet over the water! It is a bulky, careful-ly constructed cup, fashioned of grasses, sedges, moss, rootlets and rushes, lined with finer grasses and tightly tied to the surrounding vegetation with milkweed fibers.

The mother bird completes the nest in just three to six days. Within, she lays three or four pale, bluish-green eggs that are dec-orated with brown, black and purple blotches and spots, mostly at the larger end. When the babies hatch out in eleven days, they are scarlet-skinned, with a bit of grey down, blind, and so weak they can barely lift their heads. By their ninth day, they are sufficiently feath-ered to fly! The babies then resemble their mother—dusky brown and streaked to afford them good camouflage. (The male birds are a year old before they develop their red epaulets.) Each pair of birds raises two or three broods a season, and the mother bird builds a nice, new nest for each family!

The redwings have many enemies to contend with. The marsh wren may sneak into their nest and pierce the eggs with her beak. A cowbird may lay *her* egg in their nest. Eggs and nestlings are snatched by crows, hawks, owls and bitterns. The male redwing puts up a fierce fight to defend his family. By swooping and pecking at the intruder, he is often able to drive off much larger birds.

During the nesting season, much of the redwings' food is found in the marshes, where they eat weed seeds, insects and berries, but they also eat grain and seeds in newly plowed fields and some at har-vest time. In the north, they are considered to be beneficial birds, for here they take comparatively little grain and destroy many inju-rious insects, such as, the hairy larvae of tent caterpillars and gypsy moth caterpillars, (which many birds won't eat) grasshoppers, flies, weevils, ants and bugs. The good they do far outweighs the harm!

THE MAYAPPLE

The fascinating Mayapple, *Podophyllum peltatum*, is a native of Eastern North America. It is found in open forest glades, or, where meadows border woodlands, in rich moist soil.

Most woodland plants flower in the spring, before the tree leaves have fully opened, and sunlight is available to them. Thus, we find Jack-In-the-Pulpit, Spring-Beauty, Trillium, Blood-Root, and Mayapple among the first plants to leaf out.

The Mayapple is a perennial herbaceous plant. Such plants put much of their energy into producing below-ground growth. This is an adaptation that maximizes their chance of surviving the winter. Mayapples have strong, horizontal, underground stems or "rhizomes," with clusters of roots along them at intervals. At each of these root-clusters, a plant appears above the ground, soon forming a dense colony of individuals, each about a foot in height.

As the Mayapples emerge from the earth, the lobes of their leaves are folded about their stems in the manner of tightly closed umbrellas. When they are fully spread, the leaf "umbrellas," a foot in diameter, have four to nine lobes, (usually seven in number), radiating from their stems. Their upper surface is a bright iridescent green, sometimes with bronze markings; they are paler green beneath and slightly fuzzy to the touch.

In every clump of Mayapples, some stems rise into double leaves. It is surprising to see that one of these leaves is always larger than its twin! At the fork of these stems, hidden from view under the leaves, we find a tiny green bud, carried on its own little stalk. This bud opens into a cup-shaped, glistening, white flower with a yellow center. We note that there is a variable number of petals present—usually six, but sometimes as many as nine! The beautiful flower, two inches in diameter, is soon visited by that insect busy in early spring, warm in her furry, black and gold coat, the queen bumblebee. As she flies from flower to flower collecting pollen for her new family, she pollinates the Mayapple. Soon, the white petals fall and a green berry is formed. It grows larger and larger, until, by the end of the summer, it is a ripe, smooth, golden fruit about the size and shape of a hen's egg.

The belovèd American poet, James Whitcomb Riley, wrote thus of the Mayapple:

> *And will any poet sing of a lusher, richer thing*
> *than a ripe May apple, rolled like a pulpy lump of gold*
> *Under thumb and finger tips; and poured molten through the lips?"*

Our Mayapple, sometimes called "Mandrake," is a relative of the Barberry. It is not to be confused with the Mandrake of the Old World, a medicinal plant of the Nightshade family.

A drug, podophyllin, is extracted from the dried rhizome of the Mayapple. It is cathartic and purgative, and was once a frequent ingredient of patent medicines. When taken in large doses, it is toxic and may even prove to be fatal!

The Mayapple has also been called Raccoon Berry and Hog Apple because these animals seek it out, and Wild Lemon for its appearance. Mayapples are at their most delicious in the late summer when the parent plants have died down and the golden fruit has fallen to the ground.

The flavor of the Mayapple has been compared to strawberry, guava and passionfruit. It makes a delicous jam and is said to be delightful to drink when mixed with lemonade!

A CONGENIAL GARDEN COMPANION

What a fortunate gardener it is that finds a friendly toad residing near the flower bed! This chubby little creature, about four inches long, is a stupendous consumer of harmful insects. It finds cutworms and beetles, caterpillars, centipedes and millipedes, grasshoppers and flies, all to be quite delicious. It also eats snails, spiders, worms and slugs. It may even eat a hornet or a yellow jacket! In fact, a toad will attempt to eat any moving creature that is smaller than it is.

The toad has a tongue that is attached at the front of his mouth, and he is able to dart it out for quite a distance at his hapless prey. The prey sticks to the tongue and is quickly brought to the toad's large mouth. He may use his hands to push the struggling insect down his throat, then, closes his eyes blissfully while swallowing it. During the three months of summer, a single garden toad may consume up to ten thousand insects!

The toad's skin is rough and dry. It has dark spots on its back, each having one or two "warts." These warts are actually glands which secrete a milky substance that is irritating and even toxic to some who would eat it.

In Shakespeare's play, *Macbeth*, a witch recites:

> Round about the cauldron go
> In the poison'd entrails throw.
> Toad that under cold stone
> Days and nights has thirty one
> Swelter'd venom sleeping got,
> Boil thou first i' the charmed pot.....

The toad's ground color is often brown with reddish or yellow warts. Its belly is white with black spots. The females are brighter in hue, but only the males have a black throat. The toad has the ability to lighten and darken its color over a period of several hours in order to blend in with its surroundings.

The eyes of a toad are elevated, with golden, jewel-like irises, and pupils that are oval, that is, elongated left to right. When the toad sleeps, he draws in his eyes and they no longer bulge.

As the toad grows, his skin becomes too tight; it splits and he sheds it in the manner of a snake. He performs this act in a hidden place, then, sometimes, he eats the skin! The toad is then quite bright and beautiful in his new clothes.

When a toad is pursued by a predator, it will attempt to hop away, or, it may flatten itself to the ground, hoping to be overlooked. It may, instead, inflate itself, lower its head and turn itself into a hard-to-swallow ball. If seized, it may feign death, but, when actually in the mouth of a predator, it may cry out and shriek.

Among the many creatures that are immune to the toads' toxin and happily eat them are owls, hawks, crows, herons, hognose snakes, and skunks. However, the greatest mortality of toads is caused by automobiles, especially on warm rainy nights when amphibia are on their way to spawn.

In the breeding season, mid-April through May, the male American toad "sings" to attract females. He produces a musical, sustained, high-pitched trill by inflating a balloon-like air sac which is part of his throat skin and acts as a resonator.

American toads have a homing instinct, and, at the breeding season, these usually solitary creatures return in great swarms to the waters where they themselves hatched out. The female toad lays her eggs in the shallows in two long gelatinous strings which usually become wound around water plants. The tiny, jet black eggs, one millimeter in diameter, may be over eight thousand in number! (It is fortunate that there are so many, for, as soon as they are laid, they are preyed upon by fish, crawdads, water beetles, and dragonfly larvae.) The male toad fertilizes the eggs in the water, then, in three to twelve days, the tiny, almost black tadpoles emerge. They seem to consist mostly of a head with a long flat tail! The tadpoles have external gills with which to breathe in the water. They are omnivorous, eating algae, tiny bits of plants, and microscopic animals.

Over a period of about forty to sixty days, the tadpoles change into tiny toads. First, bumps appear which grow into hind legs with five webbed toes on each foot. Two weeks later, the arms begin to appear with four fingers on each hand that are not webbed. The back legs are used for propulsion, and the front for balance and keeping afloat. The tail is absorbed and the little creature begins to breathe air. It is ready to leave its home in the water for life on the land. It takes several years for the tiny toad to become mature. Although it is then a terrestrial creature, it is interesting to note that a toad never drinks with its mouth, but, lies down in shallow water and absorbs it through its skin!

The toad is a cold-blooded animal, and its body temperature tends to become nearly the same as the surrounding air. When the days become shorter and the sun's warmth weakens, food is scarce. The toad seeks out soft, moist earth. It digs with its hind legs, and pushes itself backward into the hole with its front legs. The earth collapses around it and covers it. It draws its legs up, puts it head down on its feet, and sleeps for five months or more. (Toads have a substance called glycerol in their body, which is also used in automobile antifreeze. They can have as much as thirty-five percent of their body water become ice and still survive because the "antifreeze" within their cells protects them from destruction.)

The range of the common garden toad, *Bufo americanus*, extends from the Hudson Bay in Canada, southward, through Eastern North America. It is found wherever there are cultivated fields, gardens and woodlands. If it has adequate cover, moist soil and a source of plentiful food, a toad may live a long life; in fact, captive toads have lived for over thirty years, devouring insects all the while!

THE GLORIOUS NORTHERN ORIOLE

The Northern Oriole, formerly known as the Baltimore Oriole, is a member of the blackbird family and truly American, for birds of the blackbird family are found only in the Americas. It is a graceful, beautiful bird, about eight inches in length. The male wears the colors of the English nobleman, Lord Baltimore. His head, back, and tail are glossy black and his black wings bear bright white edges. His breast, rump and shoulder patch are a brilliant, golden-orange hue. The female bird is olive-brown above and a muted yellow-orange beneath. Her dark wings have pale whitish bars. Her subtle coloration affords her camouflage at the nest. The male's gaudy colors gain the attention of females and intimidate other males.

Of all the blackbirds, orioles are considered to be the best singers. Their song is robust and rich. The sound is clear and flute-like, with single and double notes sung in short phrases. Each individual bird sings his own distinctive tune!

In early May, when the orchards are in bloom, the male orioles return to their breeding grounds, preceding the females by several days. Year after year, they return to the same site! They court the females by whistling sweet, low-pitched songs, and displaying their beautiful plumage.

The female oriole is the weaver of a wonderful nest. It is usually attached to the end of a slender, drooping branch, quite high in a tree, thus, affording some protection against climbing predators. (Once, elms were preferred for the nest site, but, with their decline, many other trees are utilized, such as maples, poplars, willows, hickories and apples.) The male bird brings nesting materials to the female, who, perching on a twig, head downward, weaves them into a pendulous sack, using her long, pointed beak as a shuttle. She works from the top down. She utilizes horsehair, milkweed fibers, grapevine bark, and pieces of string when available. The lining of the nest is of hair, wool, or soft, fine grasses. The completed nest is about five inches long, four and one-half inches wide at the bottom, and the oval entrance, usually at the top, is two to three inches across. This grayish-brown hanging pouch, whose walls are nowhere more than one-fourth inch thick, is so strong it can withstand the fierce storms of the following winter.

The oriole eggs are laid in early June. They are lovely things— pale grayish-white or bluish-white, decorated mostly at their larger ends with black and brown streaks, scrawls, and splotches, and tints of lavender and gray.

The mother bird incubates the eggs for two weeks. The protective father defends the site, daringly driving off intruders such as blue jays, grackles, mockingbirds, and red and gray squirrels.

When the young birds' feathers grow in, they all resemble their mother. The males don't develop their bright adult plumage until the following year.

The oriole is one of the most beneficial birds to man because it devours hairy, spiny, destructive caterpillars which many other birds avoid. It eats the fall webworm, spiny elm caterpillar, tussock caterpillar, forest tent caterpillar, and the gypsy moth caterpillar. (The oriole has learned to remove the hairy skin first, then eat the caterpillar!) In fact, caterpillars are the most important part of the oriole's diet. It also eats click beetles, ants, grasshoppers, scale insects, sawfly larvae, and junebugs. It enjoys eating wild fruits like mulberries, blackberries and wild cherries. You may be able to lure a nearby oriole with a special treat—half an orange pierced on a twig!

William Dean Howells wrote this of our glorious oriole:

> I know his name, I know his note
>> That so with rapture takes my soul;
> Like flame the gold beneath his throat,
>> His glossy cope is black as coal.

O oriole, it is the song

    You sing me from the cottonwood,

Too young to feel that I was young,

    Too glad to guess if life were good.

Northern Orioles spend their winter in Central and South America. In the spring, from the time they arrive in our southern states until they reach their real summer homes in the north, they travel forty-five miles a day, even when stopping frequently to rest and to eat!

THE DEVOTED ROCK DOVE

Last April, my husband and I were fortunate indeed to visit some of the cities of northern Italy. I was duly impressed by the magnificent buildings, paintings, and sculptures, and the always present feeling of great antiquity. However, in this ancient land, in countryside as well as city, man has truly conquered "Nature."

Having lived twenty-three years in Woodstock, I felt a great longing for the presence of wildlife. One afternoon, while walking about Venice, I came to a dusty plaza. I sat down on the steps of a monument to eat my luncheon roll. I was soon visited by a score of friendly pigeons, and was delighted to share my food with them. They seemed larger, healthier, and more relaxed than their relatives, introduced to the United States many years ago.

The pigeons we see in U.S. cities are generally domestic pigeons, directly descended from the Rock dove, *Columba livia*, which have become feral.

The pigeon is a stocky, medium-sized bird, about thirteen and one-half inches long. It is a soft gray color, with two narrow black wing bands, a broad black band on the end of its short, fan-like tail, and a white rump. It has amber eyes, and bright rose-colored legs and feet. As it walks, its head nods forward and back. This movement displays the beautiful, iridescent, purple, green and rose colors of the neck feathers. The call of the pigeon is a soft, gutteral coo. As it coos, the pigeon inflates its pretty throat. Over the centuries, selective breeding has given rise to many varieties of pigeons, differing in their color, shape and plumage.

The diet of pigeons consists of grain, such as corn and oats, weed seeds, fruits, berries and bugs. Pigeons drink by immersing their bills and sucking up the water! (They don't have to raise their heads, in the manner of most birds, in order for it to run down their throats.)

The ancestral Rock dove is native to northern Europe, North

Africa, and central and southern Asia. It is most plentiful along the coasts, where it nests on cliffs—on their rocky ledges, in their crevasses, and in their shallow caves. In cities and suburbs, tall buildings have taken the place of the cliffs. Pigeons also nest under bridges. For many years, a small colony of pigeons nested under the Millstream Bridge in Woodstock.

The male bird brings nesting materials, such as twigs, grasses and straw to the female, who, sitting, tucks it under herself and fashions a rather flimsy nest. Two glossy, white eggs are laid, and incubated for seventeen days by both parents. During the last days of incubation, the cells lining the parents' crops enlarge. These cells contain a creamy, white substance known as "pigeon milk," which is very rich in proteins and fats. When the baby pigeons, or squabs, hatch out, they are blind, helpless, and covered with a sparse, yellow down. They poke their soft bills into their parents' throats and the parents pump the pigeon milk into them. After five days, the parents feed the squabs grain mixed with the milk in their crops. By the time the babies are six weeks old, they are fully-feathered and ready to eat and drink by themselves.

Since pigeons are primarily grain eaters, and their babies are not fed any appreciable amount of animal food, the pigeon milk assures that they will receive adequate protein during their maximum growth period. It is thought that this method of feeding the young is what limits the number of pigeon babies to one or two in a brood.

Pigeons are prolific and can produce several broods annually. In fact, they breed to the limit of their food supplies. Their natural enemies are rats, weasels, and, of course, hawks.

Three thousand years ago, Egyptians were keeping pigeons, and Pliny speaks of Romans being ardent pigeon fanciers at the beginning of the Christian era. Knights embarking on the Crusades sometimes carried pigeons with them. From time to time, they would release a bird with a message tied to its neck or under its wing. Devotion to its mate would draw the bird home.

A current theory explaining the pigeon's ability to return home is that the pigeon navigates by responding to the earth's magnetic field!

Pigeon wings make rattling claps when the birds suddenly take flight if alarmed. Vergil wrote and Dryden translated from the Latin:

> As when a dove her rocky hold forsakes,
> Roused in a fright her sounding wings she shakes;
> The cavern rings with clattering—out she flies,
> And leaves her callow care, and cleaves the skies;
> At first she flutters: —but at length she springs
> To smoother flight, and shoots upon her wings.

THE GREAT EGRET

On the Zena Road, between the Town of Kingston and Woodstock, lies a small, beautiful reservoir with marshy borders. It provides an excellent habitat for many species of water-loving birds. Last week, when driving home from Kingston, Edward and I paused there to see what birds were present. We were excited and delighted to discover a pair of Great Egrets! These magnificent birds, actually, a species of heron, are quite large. They may be up to forty-two inches in length! Their feathers are a glistening, snowy white, and their long, straight, sharp bills are brilliant yellow. They wade through shallow water on stilt-like black legs with slender, unwebbed toes. The egrets' tails are short, their necks long, and their wings broad and powerful. They fly with a slow, regular beat, with their necks drawn back in an "S"-shape, and their legs extended behind.

Egrets are usually found in the vicinity of water. They inhabit marshy ponds, swamps, islands, the shores of lakes and rivers, and tidal flats. They are adapted for wading, and, in the shallow water, they stalk their prey. Their diet consists of fish, frogs, snakes, crayfish and insects.

The egret hunts by day. When seeking its prey, the egret stands perfectly still until the hapless creature approaches, or, it wades silently through the water, searching. When the prey is sighted, the egret thrusts out its long neck downward, seizes the creature in its long bill, tosses it up and swallows it whole. (The pointed bill is used to grasp and not as a spear.)

While most birds clean and preen their feathers with oil they have taken with their bill from a special oil gland, the egret has an additional adaptation. It produces a substance known as "powder-down" in patches on its body. This material breaks apart into dusty, absorbent particles that the bird rubs onto its feathers that are soiled with fish oil. It scrapes off the powder with its claw, then preens the feathers in the normal fashion.

During the nesting season, the Great Egret developes beautiful, finely-dissected plumes known as "aigrettes." They spring from beneath its shoulders, are twenty inches long, and may be fifty in number! These plumes were much in demand for decorating the large, elaborate women's hats of the Edwardian era. Adult birds were slaughterd on their nests by the thousands for the money the plumes would bring. The orphaned baby birds were left to starve. The same situation occurred in southern Europe concerning a sub-species of the Great Egret. When it appeared that the birds would be hunted to their extinction, protective legislation was enacted. Today, these egrets are doing quite well; they have recovered their former numbers and continue to extend their range northward and westward. In fact, the breeding range of the Great Egret extends all the way to New England!

Great Egrets become gregarious at breeding time, and usually prefer to nest in colonies—sometimes among other species of heron. The male bird chooses the nest site, which may be amidst reeds, or in a shrub or tree. It is usually placed between ten to thirty feet above ground, but may be located as much as eighty feet up! (In the North, red maple and beech trees are favored nest sites.) Both birds build the nest by bringing materials, one piece at a time, in their bills. The finished nest is a platform two feet across, and made of sticks. It may be lined with finer materials such as leaves, grasses and moss.

The eggs, usually three or four in number, are pale blue or greenish-blue. Both parents incubate them for twenty-four days. The down-covered baby birds are tended by both parents and fed with regurgitated prey.

Soon after they are able to leave the nest, the young egrets begin to wander northward. Their parents moult the long, beautiful "aigrette" feathers and fly northward as well. By early fall, many egrets are found hundreds of miles north of their nesting grounds! With the onset of cold weather, they fly southward once again.

There are plans afoot to dredge the little reservoir on Zena Road. I would hope that the authorities take into consideration the effect on resident wildlife, especially nesting waterfowl, and choose the least injurious time of year to dredge.

A WOODLAND MAJESTY

How breath-taking it is to see a magnificent white-tail buck, dark against the snow on a winter night, his large, many-pointed antlers gleaming in the moonlight!

This noble creature, shy and timid while his antlers are developing in spring and summer, becomes quite formidable during the breeding season of autumn and early winter. Does and young bucks scatter at the sight of him like leaves before the wind. The antlers which he bears so proudly are bony growths that start as "buds" on his brow in April or May. They are covered with a soft, living tissue suffused with blood vessels known as "the velvet." When the antlers have reached full size in September, they harden and their velvet covering dries. The buck rubs the velvet on saplings and brush until it peels off in tatters. As he does this, he leaves his scent and makes his presence known to other bucks in the area.

The first antlers a buck produces are usually simple spikes. In the following years, each forward-curving antler beam has tines or "points." The size of the antlers and the number of points generally increase with age, however, heredity and nutrition play a role as well.

A mature white-tail buck stands about forty inches high at the shoulder, is about six feet in length, and while the average weight is one-hundred and seventy-five pounds, some have weighed four hundred! The does are smaller; the average weight of a doe in our area being one hundred and twenty-five pounds.

In summer, the deer bear a fine-haired, glossy, chestnut-red coat, and in winter, a brownish-gray coat, thick with hollow hairs that trap air and aid in insulation. The deer's distinctive tail is brown above and fringed with white, and is pure white on its underside.

The deer have very keen senses, and are always on the look-out for predators. Although they are color-blind, they can spot the slightest movement at a very great distance. They have a good sense of smell, and their excellent hearing is enhanced by their large ears that they constantly move to direct the sound. A nervous deer will stamp its front feet and produce a startling, loud snort known as "the blow" before wheeling and running off, the signaling white flag of its tail held high.

A herd of deer bounding across a meadow is a glorious sight. They can run at forty-five miles per hour, leap twenty-seven feet horizontally, and eight and one-half feet straight up!

In the spring, after a gestation period of two hundred and ten days, the fawns are born. They are the most beautiful and charming of woodland creatures! They only weigh about five pounds, and have pretty red coats dappled with many white spots. As they sit on the ground amidst the leaves, they are very well camouflaged.

The mother deer leaves them alone most of the day and returns to nurse them every few hours. (Fawns have little or no scent in their first days of life that could attract predators such as coyotes or foxes.) Young does may stay at the side of their mother for two years, and young bucks for one year.

Deer have various external scent glands, including a gland between the two lobes of the hoof. As the deer walks, it leaves a scent on the ground. This helps deer, such as a doe and her fawn, to track one another.

Deer are most active at sunset and sunrise. Their favorite habitats are the edges of forests, woodland clearings and old fields. Here, they can find grasses, succulent herbs, leaves and mushrooms to graze upon in the summer, and the twigs, bark and fruit of bushes such as sumac and elderberry, and of young trees such as apple, cherry, maple and willow to browse in the winter. They will also stand on their hind legs to stretch up and reach for frozen apples, and dig through the snow and leaf litter for acorns. When they are very hungry, they will eat mosses and lichens.

Deer have no upper incisor teeth! When they browse a twig, its end is torn and brushy, as opposed to the clean, forty-five degree angle cut a rabbit makes.

When the cold of winter is severe and prolonged and the snow is deep, deer seeking shelter assemble in protected areas, often on a southern slope, known as "yards." They mill about, trampling down the snow in the yard and the trails leading in and out. Sometimes the snows are so heavy that they become trapped in their yards, and, after they have eaten all the available browse, they starve in great numbers. The fawns are the first to go, because, when the easily reached food is gone, they aren't big enough to stretch higher. After a severe winter, when the does have been starved, they don't produce many offspring.

Last spring, a neighbor sadly pointed out to me her gardener-tended border of exotic flowers, laid out like a Swedish smorgasbord, and browsed by grateful deer. "Who attracted deer to this neighborhood?" she wondered aloud. To which I should have answered, paraphrasing the words of a Department of Environmental Conservation offical regarding a bear situation, "Madam, the deer are not in your backyard, you are in their front yard!"

A MOST IMPRESSIVE WOODPECKER

How exciting it is to hear the wild, laughing cry of the pileated woodpecker, sounding like something in a "Tarzan" movie, and looking up, to see the bird, swaying first to the left, then to the right, on either side of the tree trunk, its red crest brilliant in the sunlight!

When you try to approach it for a better look, it takes off in an undulating flight: rising as it flaps its wings, then, descending as it folds them, it lets momentum carry it in a falling arc.

This magnificent bird is as large as a crow, clothed in plumage that is mostly black, with dashing white stripes on face and neck, and white feathers lining its wings. It is the only woodpecker in North America that has a crest!

The pileated woodpecker is specially adapted for climbing about on tree trunks and limbs, and chiseling wood in search of food. It has short legs and strong feet, with two toes in front and two in back, bearing long, sharp curved claws that can cling to bark.

The feathers at the tip of a woodpecker's tail are strong, stiff, bristly and pointed. The tail can be used as a support while the bird climbs, or, as a prop to keep it from slipping while it rests, clinging to the surface of a tree.

The woodpecker's large, handsome head is balanced on a slender neck, which, however, has very powerful muscles. The woodpecker's bill is strong, straight and chisel-like. Its surface is protected with a thick layer of horny material. As the bird props itself against a tree with its body tilted away at a slant so that it will have a greater swing with its bill, it pounds with such force that it is able to rip off heavy strips of bark, creating characteristic rectangular holes. (The woodpecker's nostrils are covered with bristle-like feathers that keep it from inhaling wood dust!)

The woodpecker's tongue is long, worm-like, and capable of being protruded to a great extent. Its tip is hard and bordered with bristles. When the bird lays open the bark with its bill, it sweeps out the ants, grubs and adult beetles that are hiding in crevices with its tongue! It can also use its tongue to spear large insects. The woodpecker dines on berries in season, and is quite fond of wild grapes.

If a female bird nests in a hole, she can be as brightly colored as the male, no need for camouflage, and so it is with a pileated woodpecker. Each year, a new hole is excavated by both woodpecker parents, and usually situated about forty-five feet above the ground, facing south or east. No nesting materials are brought in to line the deep, vertical, tunnel-like hole, which is peaked at the top and level on the bottom. There are three or four glossy white eggs, incubated by both parents. Each parent has its own hunting area; one stays at the nest, then leaves when the other arrives. The incubation period is very short—only eleven to seventeen days. The nestlings are blind, naked, and covered with sparse down. Hole nestlings are usually much noisier in the nest than nestlings in open nests, and woodpecker babies, safe in their holes, call without interruption.

The pileated woodpecker is found in mature, mixed forests of deciduous trees and conifers, throughout Eastern North America. It is solitary and a year-round resident in its range.

Once there was an even larger woodpecker inhabiting the Southern United States known as the ivory-billed woodpecker, but it is now feared to be extinct. It is a good idea to leave "snags" (dead trees) standing, to benefit cavity users such as chickadees, nuthatches, titmice, woodpeckers and even, flying squirrels!

A GIANT UNDER SIEGE

The Eastern Hemlock, *Tsuga canadensis*, is a tall, symmetrical, cone-shaped evergreen with fine, dense foliage and pendulous branches. It prefers to live in a cool, shaded spot such as a ravine or north-facing mountainside, with its roots in rocky soil moist with humus. It is often found growing amidst white pines.

The first four or five years, Eastern Hemlocks grow only an inch a year while their dense, fibrous root systems are developing, but when their growth takes off, they can reach about one hundred feet in height. In fact, the tallest Eastern Hemlock grew to one hundred and sixty feet, and the oldest lived nine hundred eighty-eight years!

Hemlock needles are very short and flattened. Each needle has its own tiny petiole, or stem. (The hemlock is the only conifer whose needles have stems.) Mature needles are deep green and glossy on their upper surface, and pale green beneath, striped lengthwise with two white lines. New greenish-yellow needles appear at the end of the twigs in June.

In May, tiny, green pistillate flowers develop at the end of each twig, while yellow, ball-like, pollen-bearing flowers form along their sides. Soon the beautiful trees are decorated with dainty reddish-brown cones that dangle from every branch tip. The seeds in the cones are greatly appreciated by overwintering, seed-eating birds, and are the favorite food of the feisty red squirrel.

Hemlocks begin to produce cones when they are about twenty years old, and can continue to produce them for more than four hundred and fifty years!

Hemlock bark, reddish-brown and ridged with furrows, is rich in tannin and was once in great demand by the leather tanning industry. It was said that the bark "slipped," that is, could be removed from the logs only in the spring and summer months. After the trees were felled, their trunks were girdled at four-foot intervals, then, vertical cuts were made so that the bark could be removed in four-foot rectangular pieces. The pieces of bark were stacked and left to dry in the woods. The following winter, after an accumulation of snow, the bark could be hauled out by an ox team and sledge.

In Woodstock, this "tanbark" was hauled to the Tannery Brook, where, according to our town historian, Alf Evers, one John C. Ring had a tan house and tan vats. After local animals were slaughtered, the hides were treated there and the finished leather sold to shoemakers and harnessmakers.

Tanneries mixed oak bark with the hemlock bark, because the hemlock bark imparted a bright reddish hue to the leather, which was modified by the brown dye from the oak.

The tannin in hemlock bark is curative. The Native Americans boiled and pounded the bark into a paste, then made it into a poultice for burns and wounds. The resin and the oil of hemlock, distilled from the needles, are antiseptic.

Hemlock wood is brittle and cross-grained. It has two useful characteristics: it doesn't split while being nailed, and it grasps nails and spikes very tightly. It was once used extensively for railroad ties and for the larger beams in the frames of houses and barns.

The hemlock trees in the Hudson Valley are under siege by a formidable insect foe. It is known as the woolly adelgid. This creature was introduced from Asia to the Pacific Northwest in 1924. It appeared in Virginia in the 1950s and moved slowly northward.

Woolly adelgids produce a white cottony substance that covers their bodies. The presence of cottony masses on the needles, twigs and bark of hemlocks means that adelgids are present. The adelgids suck a tree's sap from its young twigs. The tree weakens and drops its needles prematurely. Total defoliation may occur, with the resulting death of the tree.

Individual specimen trees are treated with horticultural oils or soap compounds in an effort to smother the insects, but thick stands of trees are being lost. Researchers are working to identify and import the adelgid's natural enemies to save our magnificent hemlocks!

A SPECTRAL PRESENCE

Late one night, many years ago, my husband, Edward, was walking from the New York Central commuter train stop at Briarcliff Manor to his home. He was taking a short-cut through Waldheim woods, deep in thought, when he was quite startled by several unearthly screams. Looking about for their source, he spotted a crow-sized bird, pale in the moonlight. When it turned its ghastly, ghostly face towards him, he realized it was a barn owl!

The barn owl's coal-black eyes glare from the center of a facial disk of radiating, white feathers; the whole face is outlined by a heart-shaped ring of brown. The feathers on its back and the outside of its wings are patterned with light buff-brown and gray, and the feathers of its underparts are white with tiny dark dots. The wings are edged with down and so soft that the owl is able to fly soundlessly.

The barn owl has long, slender, completely feathered legs, equipped with strong, curved talons with which to seize its prey. It also has a hooked bill partially hidden in the feathers of its facial disk, with which to tear into that prey.

Owls see well by day and by night. Their large, forward-facing eyes are almost immobile in the sockets, but the birds can turn their heads around a considerable distance. In fact, some species can turn their heads 270 degrees! Owls' sense of hearing is quite acute, and they depend on it to pinpoint the location of their prey.

The barn owl's food consists almost entirely of small, ground-living rodents such as rats, mice and voles that are harmful to farm and garden crops. Owls tend to swallow their prey whole, rather than tear it into pieces as do hawks. They clutch a hapless rodent in one foot and bring it up to the beak while bending towards it. Owls are far-sighted and can't see well up close, so, they make use of "whiskers" around their mouths that can be raised to help them examine their food and position it for swallowing, head first!

By a rotating movement of the owl's stomach, the nutritious elements of the food are extracted and the indigestible portions, such as bones, hair, feathers and claws, are rolled into balls known as owl pellets, which are brought up and expelled through the mouth.

The barn owl frequents ruins and neglected cemeteries. It loves old towers, and in the 1890s, barn owls nested in the northwestern tower of the Smithsonian Institution in central Washington, D.C. It nests in church belfries, barn lofts, the attics of old buildings, hollow trees and holes in embankments. It doesn't build an actual nest, but lays five to ten chalky, white eggs placed on a base of its pellets, on bare wood or even stone. Only the mother bird incubates the eggs, but she is fed on the nest by her devoted mate. She lays an egg every day or two, and begins to incubate each egg as soon as it is laid, so, the babies hatch at different times and vary greatly in size.

After a long incubation of thirty-two to thirty-four days, the babies hatch out with their eyes and ears closed and their bodies covered with a fluffy white down. Both parent birds care for the young, but, if there isn't enough food, the young hatchlings may fall prey to their older siblings.

When there is available food, the barn owls can breed in any season, even winter! If food is scarce, they will produce fewer eggs or will not breed at all.

The barn owl inhabits all the continents except Antarctica. It is a year round resident in its home range. In the Americas, it is found from southern Canada southward to Tierra Del Fuego.

UNTIL DEATH DO THEY PART

The subtle beauty of a lichen is readily apparent, but its wondrous, true nature is not. What appears to be a plant is actually a partnership of two or three very different organisms inhabiting one body! One partner is always a fungus and the other is an alga, a cyanobacterium, or both. The fungus can't make its own food, but the alga or cyanobacterium conducts photosynthesis, that is, it can make energy-rich food compounds out of carbon dioxide, water and sunlight. The fungus supplies water and minerals, and furnishes a protective coating over an internal layer where the alga and the cyanobacterium reside.

Lichens grow on rocks, tree trunks, sand and soil. When environmental conditions become too severe, lichens can slow down metabolically, thus, they can survive extremes of heat, cold and drought. Lichens live on sunbaked rocks in the desert and windswept cliffs in the mountains. They are found in both Polar regions; in fact, in the Arctic, they occur submerged in icy seawater!

One thing that lichens must have in order to flourish is clean air. Their bodies absorb water from rain, mist and dew, and with it any pollution that may be present. They are especially sensitive to sulphur dioxide and fluorine and are often very scarce in the vicinity of large cities.

Lichens are extremely vulnerable to the destruction of their habitat. An area with a great diversity of lichens indicates an undisturbed ecosystem, such as that of an ancient forest. Scientists, noting the presence of many species of lichen, can identify an area that is still pristine and a treasure that should be protected.

Lichens are pioneers. The fungal partner in a lichen gives off an acid that eats into rock, enabling the lichen to anchor itself, for it has no true roots, stems or leaves. Once it gains a foothold on a rock, it continues to etch the surface with acids. Particles are loosened allowing the entry of water, which further disintegrates the rock, helping to create soil. As a lichen dies, its tissues are left with the decomposing mineral fragments, making a more fertile soil suitable for mosses, ferns or more highly evolved plants.

Lichens are usually classified as crustose, which are "crusty," foliose, which are "leaflike," and fruiticose, which are "shrubby." An example of a crustose lichen is the beautiful "map lichen," which forms greenish-yellow or bright orange patterns on rocks throughout North America. Sometimes, the very same rock may bear "boulder lichen," which is a foliose lichen that forms rosettes that are several inches wide. Its light green body bears tiny craters that are chocolate-brown within. These are the reproductive organs of the fungal partner. Another foliose lichen that is common in Woodstock is the Pale Shield Lichen, a grayish-green lichen that thickly covers the furrowed bark on the trunks of ash trees.

The most exciting and beautiful lichens, to me, are the fruiticose lichens. They are slender, branched and either hang or stand erect. On Goat Hill Road, in Saugerties, among the layered bluestone outcroppings, there are British Soldiers, Pyxie Cups, and Ladder Lichen.

British Soldiers have one inch tall greenish-gray bodies bearing the brightest red fruiting tips! They grow on the soil, amidst pine needles and forest detritus. Right beside them are the Pyxie Cups that look like goblets for tiny elves and fairies! The Ladder Lichen has cups arising from the center of cups, forming tiers up to three inches high.

Old Man's Beard is an aptly named fruiticose lichen found throughout North America. It forms hairlike tufts that hang from twigs or rocks and may be several inches in length.

Lichens have economic importance as the source of dyes. They are traditionally used to color Harris tweeds! Dye extracted from lichens is used to color litmus paper, an important chemical indicator. Usnic acid, used in antibiotic salves, is found in Old Man's Beard Lichen.

Reindeer Moss, which is actually a lichen, is a very important food for reindeer and caribou during the harsh Arctic winter. Some birds, such as Ruby-throated Hummingbirds, and Red-eyed Vireos, make use of lichens when building and camouflaging their beautiful nests.

Lichens grow very slowly, sometimes increasing in size less than one millimeter per year, and they live in their place for hundreds, even *thousands* of years. Some Arctic lichens are claimed to be 4,500 years old!

A BROWN VELVET BEAUTY *in the* MARSH

The common cattail, *Typha latifolia*, is found throughout the continental United States, from Newfoundland to Alaska, and southward into Mexico. It is a hardy, perennial reed that makes its home in marshes, swamps, ditches and the shallow edges of ponds and slow streams.

The cattail is a tall plant that may reach eight feet in height. The central flower stalk is stiff and straight, and the long flat leaves that sheath it bend into graceful curves in the wind.

The upper portion of the flower stalk bears a golden-yellow club-like spike of male flowers, and directly below it, a cylinder of very densely packed female flowers that has the appearance of a brown velvet sausage!

In the spring, great, golden-yellow, powdery clouds of pollen are shed by the male flowers above and fall down upon the female flowers below. The female flowers produce small downy seeds which float away on the wind.

Cattails also reproduce by "cloning." They have a rhizome (rootstock) that grows forward and sends up a number of shoots; each shoot will be a new cattail.

Cattails provide an excellent survival food source. There is no need ever to starve in a cattail swamp! In early spring, the tender young shoots may be peeled, and their white cores eaten raw in a salad or boiled in the manner of asparagus. In May and June, the immature flower spikes may be boiled and eaten as is corn on the cob. Later in the spring, the bright yellow pollen produced by the male flowers may be collected and mixed with wheat flour, and baked into pancakes and muffins!

At any season, the cores of the rhizomes may be ground into a nutritious flour that contains up to thirty percent sugar and starch. In fact, the food value is said to be equivalent to that of corn or rice.

In fall and winter, the dormant sprouts that will become next year's cattails are found on the rhizomes. These may be enjoyed eaten raw or as a cooked vegetable.

Besides their use as a food source, cattails have provided us with many useful products. The flat, narrow, sword-shaped leaves are easily woven into mats, baskets and chair seats. These leaves were once used to place between the staves and in the seams of barrel heads. Even today, cattail leaves are used in Europe for thatching roofs.

The fluffy, silky down that surrounds the seeds was used by the Indians to stuff their moccasins for warmth. It has even been used to stuff pillows and mattresses. The pollen of cattails is highly inflammable and was once used in the production of pyrotechnics and artificial stage lightning! Cattail pulp can be made into paper or rayon. Fermented cattail flour can be made into ethyl alcohol and cattail materials can be processed into chicken feed!

A cattail stand affords shelter and food for many forms of wildlife. Swans and ducks, coots, rails, grebes and bitterns all incorporate pieces of cattail into their nests. Redwinged blackbirds and yellow-headed blackbirds, swamp sparrows and marsh wrens weave their nests among the cattail stalks and leaves.

Muskrats build their lodges of cattail materials, and indeed, the cattail rhizomes and young shoots are their most important food. Beavers and geese enjoy them as well. Tiny cattail seeds are much appreciated by hungry painted turtles!

Cattails and other reeds and rushes, slowly, over time, encroach upon and dry up ponds. Then beautiful wild flowers, such as roses, asters, goldenrod and daisies will abound in the resulting meadow!

A DAINTY VAMPIRE

Mosquitoes are very successful insects, for they have adapted to life in ecosystems ranging from the Arctic Circle to the tropics!

The harmless male mosquito has a simple mouth which cannot bite through skin. He lives on plant juices and is sometimes a pollinator of flowers. His feathery antennae are bushier than those of the female mosquito. They are excellent hearing organs that perceive her high-pitched whining song produced by rapidly beating wings, and help him to locate her.

The female mosquito has piercing and sucking mouthparts. She needs to suck the blood of a bird or mammal at least once to produce her eggs. When she bites a person with a disease, such as malaria or yellow fever, she takes up the germs with the blood. They are present in her saliva when she bites her next victim, and are injected into its body. At the very least, the foreign proteins in the mosquito's saliva produce the familiar allergic reaction of an itchy spot that may become infected from scratching.

A mother mosquito lays one to three hundred eggs glued together as a little floating raft. When the babies, known as "wrigglers," are ready, they break through the bottoms of the eggs into the water. They hang heads down and tails up, munching on algae. At the end of a wriggler's tail there are two tubes. One brings air into its body and the other has finger-like projections that help it to swim along in a jerky fashion.

When a wriggler becomes a pupa to undergo metamorphosis into an adult mosquito, it breathes through two tubes on its thorax and swims by moving leaf-like projections at the end of its body. (This is very unusual, for most insects have pupae that are at rest.) When metamorphosis is complete, the skin splits on a pupa's back and the adult mosquito emerges. It rests on the floating skin until its wings dry out and it can fly away.

In the past, many swamps were drained so that mosquitoes wouldn't have access to still water for their eggs and larvae. Now, we realize the importance of swamps and wetlands as habitats for many fish, birds and other animals. Wetlands also act as giant "sponges" absorbing floodwater runoff.

DDT was once sprayed on outer house walls with impunity, causing birds who ingested insects containing the insecticide to lay soft-shelled eggs with dead babies within. DDT has also had deleterious estrogenic effects on humans. Today, the aerial spraying of Malathion to kill mosquitoes that may be carrying West Nile Virus is not accepted as harmless to humans by all scientists.

There are many natural controls on the mosquito population. Predacious aquatic insects such as dragonfly nymphs devour mosquito larvae. They are relished by sunfish, minnows and sticklebacks. Frogs and toads eat mosquitoes and so do many birds such as phoebes, barn swallows and purple martins. A single bat may capture and consume 600 mosquitoes in a single hour! (Bat houses are available to the homeowner in our area through the Cornell Cooperative Extension.)

There are many generations of the common house mosquito produced each year from spring through fall, with the final generation overwintering as adults in protected places such as attics or basements. On warm days in winter, out they come dancing madly in a cluster in the air!

A GLORIOUS GROSBEAK

Edward and I have just returned from Italy, that ancient land renowned for its charming people, delicious food, art and antiquities, but, where are its birds? I fear that most of them are long gone. Our trip culminated in Cosenza, a town in the deep south, where swallows made desultory and ineffectual attempts to reduce the mosquito population, the most dejected of pigeons sprawled upon the sidewalks, and no English sparrow could be found in the parks. Even fewer birds were noted in the countryside.

Imagine our delight, the day after our return, to see a magnificent, male, rose-breasted grosbeak at the birdfeeder! The gorgeous bird, about the size of a starling, had a glossy, jet-black head, back and tail. His black wings were crossed with white bars, his underparts were snowy white, and on his chest he bore a crimson shield-shaped patch! We saw beneath his lifted wings pretty rose-colored feathers. He had a heavy, conical bill, similar to that of the cardinal and ideally formed for cracking open seeds.

Soon, he was joined by his mate, modestly clad in pale buff plumage, heavily streaked with brown. She had white bars on her wings, and white eyebrows and chin stripes. Her under-wings were light sulphur yellow. She rather resembled an overgrown sparrow!

Rose-breasted grosbeaks prefer to inhabit thickets in deciduous woodlands, old orchards and pastures, the edges of fields, suburban parks, and wherever there is a mixture of shrubs and trees. They are of great benefit to the farmer, for they devour many harmful insects. In fact, they are sometimes called "the potato bug bird!" They relish eating caterpillars, grubs, beetles, flies and wasps. Their strong bills break open weed seeds, and they partake of wild fruits when they are available.

Not only is the rose-breasted grosbeak beautiful, it is blessed with a rich, melodious song, like a sweet, clear, rolling warble. One is more apt to hear the bird than to see him, for he likes to sing perched high in a treetop hidden by the leaves. The female bird has a pretty song also, though shorter and softer than her mate's. A strange fact concerning these birds is that they will sing during the night!

During courtship, two male birds may compete by singing to a female at the same time in order to win her affection. When she has made her choice, she and the male bird build a nest in the fork of a low tree or a shrub. The result is a flimsy affair—a cup of twigs and plant fibers, so loosely constructed that sometimes the eggs can be seen right through it from below! The eggs, usually four in number, are pale greenish-blue, beautifully spotted and blotched with purple and brown, and often capped and wreathed with these dark markings at the larger end.

The birds take turns sitting on the eggs. When the female is sitting, her affectionate, attentive mate will bring her food. Curiously, either bird may burst into song while sitting on the nest! (It would seem that such a habit might get the attention of a predator.)

As we would expect, this devoted father helps feed his young. The baby birds resemble their brown-streaked mother, but the males have a pinkish patch on their breasts and pinkish wing linings. They retain this plumage until the following spring.

The rose-breasted grosbeaks appear in New York in May, stay throughout the summer, then leave in September for their winter homes in Central and South America.

Sadly, the Audubon Society's Breeding Birds Survey of 1979 to 1994 indicated a significant decrease in the rose-breasted grosbeak populations across New York State. Reasons for this may include habitat loss, toxins in the environment, and even, roaming house cats!

AN ENTICING ROADSIDE BEAUTY

How beautiful it is to see a field of ripe milkweeds, their fuzzy, gray pods bursting open and the pearly down parachutes bearing brown seed cargos glistening in the fall sunlight!

Stands of the common milkweed, *Asclepias syriaca*, can be found growing along roadsides, the edges of woods, in fields, open meadows and waste areas. They are perennial flowering plants that arise from deeply buried rhizomes. They have strong straight stems that may reach five feet in height. All along the stem, large, oval leaves grow opposite one another in pairs. (If the bottom pair of leaves faces East and West, the pair above it faces North and South, and onward up the stem the pairs proceed in that manner.)

All parts of the plant—stems, leaves and flowers, exude a sticky, milky, latex-like juice when broken. This juice is very bitter and contains toxic chemicals. Livestock only eat milkweed if they have nothing else, and then it may poison them.

One creature that thrives on a diet of milkweed is the caterpillar of the monarch butterfly. It stores the toxic chemicals of the sap in its exoskeleton, making it poisonous to birds. The viceroy butterfly, which would be a good food for birds, closely mimics the appearance of the monarch!

Native Americans and country people have been able to make use of milkweed as a food by boiling young shoots and buds with several changes of water to remove their toxins. (Care must be taken not to confuse shoots of milkweed with the very poisonous dogbane!)

Right at the top of the tall, straight milkweed stem is a magnificent inflorescence. It is a cluster of twenty to one hundred pendulous purple flowers. These flowers give forth an intoxicating aroma, so sweet and heavy it is almost overwhelming. On a warm, bright summer day, the air around a milkweed patch is filled with the excited humming of insects.

Milkweed flowers have a complex structure. They are divided into five equal parts, each of which has a "hood" that projects upward. At the base of each hood, nectar is secreted. There also, are hidden the pollen sacs. These may hook onto the leg of a visiting insect and be carried to another flower. Unfortunately, some insects pay a sacrificial penalty. Burdened with pollen sacs, they are unable to extricate their legs from the flower and die there. Others are too heavy to fly away, and fall prey to clever spiders who have spread their webs beneath the milkweed flowers!

Milkweeds produce interesting, fuzzy seed pods up to five inches in length, decorated with rows of bumps. Within, there are deep brown seeds arranged in a shingle-like overlapping manner. Attached to each seed, is a tuft of long, silky, white hairs. In the fall, the gray pods split open along one side and the milkweed down enables the seeds to float away on the wind.

During World War I, the kapok imported to stuff ships' life preservers could not be obtained, so milkweed down was used as a substitute. Children were paid a penny for each pod they collected!

Milkweeds were once considered to be outstanding medicinal plants. Their roots were utilized by Native Americans and settlers to cure diseases of the lungs. In fact, the genus name of the common milkweed, Asclepias, refers to the Greek god of medicine, Asclepius. The Swedish father of modern plant taxonomy, Carl von Linne (Linnaeus), named the plant species "syriaca" in the 1700s, because he thought, erroneously, that the species had been brought to Europe from Syria rather than eastern North America!

A TWIG *with* LEGS

One recent, bright fall day, I crossed the little creek to look for something in our old duck barn in the woods, now used as a storage shed. As I pulled open the low door, I noticed, right at eye level, caught in a mass of cobwebs, a weird and wonderful creature. I had found the rarely seen today Northern Walking Stick insect.

A walking stick insect has a very long, very slender, cylindrical body. It has three pairs of long, slender legs, similar in form. It has a tiny head bearing long antennae, two-thirds the length of its body.

This creature is remarkable because of its excellent camouflage strategy. It moves very slowly and stealthily, often remaining motionless for long periods of time and appearing to be dead. It rests by day then feeds by night. When a walking stick believes it is in danger, it stretches out, extends its front legs and antennae in line with its body, and, with its grayish-brown color, looks exactly like a dead twig!

Lizards and rodents do sometimes manage to find and eat walking sticks, as do many species of birds. Even their close cousins, the ferocious praying mantises, devour them! (Whereas, walking sticks use their camouflage to hide from predators, mantises use theirs to hide from the prey they wish to ambush and capture!)

Walking sticks are strict vegetarians. The immature walking sticks dine on the leaves of raspberry and blackberry brambles, shrubs, and understory trees such as wild black cherry. As they mature, they move upward into the canopy of hardwoods to eat the leaves of walnuts, hazelnuts, locusts and especially, oaks.

Although walking sticks usually don't cause much damage, in the late eighteen hundreds, in Illinois, there was such a proliferation of walking sticks that they caused a severe defoliation of the oak trees, then hung from the bare twigs in large clusters. What a disturbing sight that must have been!

When a mother walking stick lays her eggs, one by one, a hundred in number, they fall to the ground with a sound like raindrops. Some eggs remain in the leaf litter, but others are carried off by a certain species of ant to their nests. The ants protect the eggs. They eat an edible appendage on the egg known as the capitulum, but the eggs still hatch out normally!

The baby walking sticks, known as nymphs, are tiny, green copies of the adults. They have a very special ability: if they should lose a leg, they can regenerate a new one!

As the walking sticks grow, they "moult," that is, they hang down from a twig, split their skin and emerge a somewhat larger creature. After five or six moults, the walking stick attains its impressive size of four inches in length!

I carefully removed the dead walking stick from our duck barn door and brought it into the house. I planned to study it, and then keep it in a box laid out on cotton. I set the creature down on the kitchen table, and noticed that its first pair of legs pointed straight forward. I took a toothpick and gently moved the legs into a more pleasing configuration, then left the room. When I returned, I glanced at the specimen and noticed that the front legs now seemed to jut up at a sharper angle. But I thought, perhaps, this was a muscle reflex of a very recently dead insect that had been prodded. I decided to arrange its legs again and its antennae as well. This final indignity was too much for the "dead" walking stick. It twirled its antennae rapidly and walked across the kitchen table in search of a tree trunk to climb. The best it could find was a can of pinto beans which it scaled, then froze. I was truly astonished! I picked up the can quite gingerly, for, although walking stick insects are harmless, I felt an atavistic reluctance for having an almost four inch long insect walk up my forearm. I put the can in a cardboard box with a screen over it to show to Edward, when he would return from the city that night.

After he had duly admired the walking stick, he took it into the woods, where it ambled down the path toward its ancestral oak tree!

OUR GOOD FRIEND DOWNY

Have you ever seen a very tiny woodpecker, no larger than an English sparrow, come eagerly to your winter feeding station in the cheerful company of chickadees, titmice, nuthatches and cardinals? It is our smallest and friendliest woodpecker, the "Downy."

The Downy is quite striking in appearance, with the sharp contrast of its black and white feathers, offset, in the male, with a scarlet patch at the back of the head. A broad white stripe runs down the bird's back from its shoulders to its rump. The wedge-shaped tail has black central feathers and outer feathers that are white barred with black. The wings are black above, bearing six bands of large, white spots, and are white beneath. The throat and breast feathers are white as well. This is a very eye-catching little bird!

Downy woodpeckers inhabit open, mixed woods, old farmlands, orchards, roadside shade trees, parks and dooryards. They range from Alaska, throughout Canada, all the way to our Southern states. Because of their special physical adaptations for food gathering in the trees, they are able to be year-round residents in New York State.

The Downy can prop itself against a tree by pushing its tail, whose feathers are equipped with bristling sharp tips, against the bark. Each foot has two toes that point forward and two backward, which gives the foot a pincer-like ability to cling.

The bird has a strong, chisel-shaped bill with which it can pry under bark and strike and drill into the wood until it reaches the hidden insect. Now comes the exciting part! How does the bird retrieve the insect from a hole too small to admit its bill? He possesses an extraordinarily long tongue, which lies soft, crumpled and worm-like when it rests in his mouth, but which can stiffen and protrude to a great length. This tongue has a hard tip, bordered with backward-slanting barbs. It is used to spear the insect. The tongue is also covered with a sticky, glue-like substance that aids in drawing out the prey.

(Bristle-like feathers protect the Downy's nostrils from inhaling too much wood dust while he chisels!)

Our tiny Downy is worth its weight in gold to the forester, farmer and orchardist. Its favorite foods are the borer insects of apple, birch and maple trees. It eats aphids, gall insects, the coddling moth, and the pine weevil. Although over seventy percent of its diet is insects, it also eats the berries of poison ivy, sumac and dogwood, and even pokeberries!

The voice of the Downy is often described as a descending rattle, and sometimes, he utters a quiet "pik" sound. He has no beautiful song with which to attract a mate. Instead, the energetic little creature drums on a resonant dry branch, sometimes for hours, to advertise his presence. James Whitcomb Riley described this drumming as "Weeding out the lonesomeness."

Both Downy parents excavate the nest cavity, usually in dead wood at a height of three to fifty feet above the ground. The opening is always a perfect circle, one and one-fourth inches in diameter. The hole goes straight in for several inches, then turns downward for eight to ten inches. At the bottom, on a bed of very fine wood chips, the mother bird lays four to six porcelain-white eggs. The parents take turns incubating the eggs by day, but all night long, only the male incubates! In twelve days the babies hatch; they are naked and blind. Both parents then work hard to provide food for their young.

Now that it is winter, tie a piece of suet to a branch of a tree that you wish to protect. First, your Downies will happily eat the offering, then, they will carefully examine every crack and crevice in the bark for hidden insect pests. The male bird tends to feed in the top of the tree and the female in the mid to lower levels. Further, the male's bill is larger and stronger and he is more apt to chisel deeply for insects, while the female is likely to use her shorter bill to pry under the bark. In this manner they can share their food resources without competition!

THERE ARE TIGERS *in the* FLOWER BEDS!

The scientific name of our Eastern Tiger Swallowtail butterfly is *Papilio glaucus*. *Papilio* is the Latin word for butterfly, and Glaucus, a son of the Lycian king Hippolochus, wore golden armor in the battle of Troy.

This beautiful butterfly is the largest on our continent. It has huge, bright yellow wings edged in black and crossed with velvety black bars. The hind wings bear long, tail-like, black extensions, and are decorated near their edges with red and blue dots. The gorgeous creature, gleaming in the sunlight, resembles a work of art executed in stained glass! (The colors on the wings are due to the presence of tiny, overlapping pigmented or prismatic scales that are easily rubbed off.)

Swallowtails fly by day, in a swift erratic pattern, in order to elude predators. When at rest, they fold their wings vertically, over their backs.

There is a large, globular, compound eye on either side of a butterfly's head. It has thirty-four thousand minute hexagonal facets that each register an image! The butterfly has a pair of knobbed antennae which have remarkable properties. They enable the insect to smell and to communicate with others of its kind. They help it to maintain its sense of balance; in fact, it can't fly without them!

The mouth parts of a butterfly are modified into a long, coiled tube known as a proboscis, which enables it to suck up flower nectar, fermenting tree sap, and the liquid from decaying fruit. Swallowtails are attracted to puddles, where they frequently gather in large numbers to drink water that contains mineral salts. Because Tiger Swallowtails fly by day, they are attracted to bright flowers, particularly pink or purple ones with large flower heads. They are partial to dining on the nectar of dame's rocket, Joe Pye weed, phlox, butterfly bush, lilac, bee-balm, New England aster, thistle, milkweed and clover.

Within the two week life span of the adult butterfly, it must find a mate. The female then lays several hundred spherical eggs, one at a time, placed upon plants that will be suitable food for the hatching-out larvae known as caterpillars.

Hatched by the warmth of the sun, a ravenous swallowtail caterpillar munches with powerful jaws on the leaves of wild cherry, poplar, birch, ash and tulip trees. It eats so much that within a month it increases its weight nearly ten thousand times!

As it grows, the caterpillar becomes too large for its skin. It stops eating and rests, then the skin behind its head splits open and it creeps out. This "moulting" occurs four or five times. The caterpillar eventually becomes a smooth, green creature with orange and black bands and blue dots that is about two and one-half inches in length. It bears two large, orange, false eye spots with black "pupils" that may have a protective function in frightening off parasitic insects, such as ichneumon wasps.

When the caterpillar is frightened, it thrusts out from behind its head two orange or yellow, fleshy "horns" that bear scent glands and give forth a sickening odor. When not feeding, the caterpillar rests upon a silken mat it weaves and stretches across a rolled leaf.

The fully developed swallowtail caterpillar spins a halter of silk around its waist which holds it upright against a support. It sheds its last caterpillar skin to reveal the angular chrysalis. The chrysalis is camouflaged in mottled brown colors to resemble a dried leaf. The miraculous change known as metamorphosis takes place within. The body of a crawling worm-like creature changes into that of a magnificent flying one.

When it is ready, the butterfly exerts pressure and breaks out of the chrysalis skin that encases it. It is weak and damp; its velvety wings crumpled. After a period of rest, it pumps fluid through the veins in its wings and they expand and dry. The swallowtail butterfly, now a mature insect known as an imago, is ready to seek sustenance and a mate and continue its ancient life cycle.

A SINGING CAT *in the* HEDGEROW

The "gray catbird," *Dumetella carolinensis,* is a member of the mockingbird family, which also includes the thrashers.

The catbird is slender, and at nine inches in length, somewhat smaller than a robin. It has a long, fan-shaped tail, rather short wings, and a long, narrow, slightly curved bill. The catbird's satiny plumage is a dark, slate-gray on its back and a lighter gray on its underparts. Its head has a black cap and under its black tail is a distinct, chestnut patch at the base. The bird's bill and legs are black as well.

The adult male and female catbirds and the juveniles are all very similar in appearance, although the babies have stubbier tails.

The gray catbird is a sociable creature, often found inhabiting shrubs, vines and hedges near houses. Sometimes, the birds, hidden in a bush, will utter a call that sounds very much like a "miaow," hence his name. If one calls back to the bird in imitation, it will respond, and jump out into view!

The catbird also sings beautiful, bubbling successions of musical notes, and reproduces phrases of other birds' songs in the manner of its southern cousin, the mockingbird. While singing, the catbird likes to flick its tail and gesture with its wings as though performing for an audience!

Catbirds are primarily insectivorous, and their presence is a great benefit to the home gardener. They particularly enjoy eating the destructive cutworm, and are adroit in the capture of moths. They also dine upon wild berries in early Autumn, such as those of the spicebush, dogwood, sassafras and Virginia Creeper. These berries are not sweet, and do not appeal to mammals. Instead, they are sour, with a high fat content; they are just right to nourish birds about to migrate for long distances!

Catbirds return to the same neighborhood year after year to raise their families. (This behavior is advantageous because foraging is safer and more efficient when birds are familiar with the terrain.)

John Burroughs writes an anecdote concerning a friend of his who had a pair of catbirds return three years in a row to her property. She had taught them to enter the window, perch on the back of a chair and take butter from a fork!

The male and female catbirds both work at building their bulky nest. Its rough exterior is woven of twigs, strips of bark, coarse grasses and leaves. It may incorporate bits of paper and rags when the birds can find them. The cup-like interior of the nest is lined with tiny rootlets and soft shredded bark.

The nest is usually concealed in a dense bush, hedge or low tree. The mother bird lays four to six glossy, dark greenish-blue eggs, and incubates them for about two weeks. (If a brown-headed cowbird lays her egg in the nest, the catbird will simply pitch it out!)

The catbird parents are very nervous birds, constantly on the lookout for enemy intruders. They are very aggressive in their defense of the nest, and will strike continuously at people, cats and dogs in an effort to drive them away. They are so zealous in this endeavor that they will even drive enemies away from the nests of other bird species!

After the mother and father catbird raise one brood of nestlings, fed solely on animal matter, they begin a second brood the same season in the same vicinity. Many, many insect pests are thus destroyed!

The gray catbird generally arrives in our area in early May, and leaves us in late October. It ranges as far north as Canada in the summer, and in winter, is found as far south as Panama.

THE GLORIOUS AMERICAN CHESTNUT
SHALL ARISE ONCE AGAIN!

Until the early 1900s, our eastern, southern and midwestern forests were graced with millions of noble trees—the magnificent American Chestnuts. They were usually found on the south or east-facing slopes of hills, in rocky or gravely, well-drained glacial soils. They grew in mixed forests among oaks, maples, hickories and birches.

These beautiful, symmetrical trees could reach one hundred feet in height and ten feet in diameter! Their massive, horizontal limbs spread wide, as noted in a line from Longfellow's 19th century poem, "The Village Blacksmith,"

Under the spreading chestnut tree
the village smithy stands.

American Chestnuts were vigorous, rapidly growing trees that reproduced by the bountiful production of nuts and new trees sprouting from the roots of a "mother tree." They were so successful that they were often the dominant tree species in their ecosystem.

The grayish-brown bark of the American Chestnut is divided by shallow fissures into broad, irregular ridges. The smaller branches are smooth and reddish and the leaf buds are dark brown.

In late June or early July, a wonderful thing occurs! Pale yellow starry flowers burst forth and cover the trees. Because the flowers appear in the summer, they cannot be nipped by frost. That is why our chestnut trees produced such an abundance of delicious, sweet nuts. The first frost causes the prickly burs that hold the nuts to burst open, allowing easy access to the nutritious food within.

Our American Chestnut was the best lumber-producing chestnut species in the world. It grew tall quickly, with straight trunks and a straight grain in the wood. The wood was brown, coarse, soft and easily worked. It had one characteristic that was legendary: it had great resistance to rot because of its high content of tannic acid. Therefore, it was utilized for railroad ties, fence posts, telegraph, then telephone poles, log cabins, shingles and caskets. It made fine furniture and firewood.

The tannic acid in the chestnut bark and heartwood was so important to the leather-producing industry (for the tanning of hides) that some major timber operations became subsidiaries to leather companies.

The American Chestnut afforded such a deep, cool shade, and was so admired for its beauty, that it was often planted around village squares, along roadsides, or on rural homesteads.

In 1904, disaster struck. A blight was discovered on chestnut trees at the New York Zoological Garden, probably brought in on Chinese chestnut trees introduced as nursery stock. The aggressive fungus would enter a tree through cracks and wounds in the tree's bark. Once it girdled the trunk, sap could not flow to the leaves and the tree died.

The fungus spores were carried by wind and rain and the disease spread like wildfire. All the mature chestnut trees were killed above the soil, however, their roots were not harmed by the fungus and saplings could sprout from them.

Today, we find groups of these "sprouts," usually two or three, that may achieve twenty feet in height before succumbing to the fungus. These saplings only rarely produce flowers and nuts. The Brooklyn Botanical Garden has been cross-breeding these flowering trees, hoping to produce a blight-resistant tree.

It has recently been found that injecting a non-virulent strain of the blight into diseased trees weakens the original blight, puts the trees into "remission" and allows them to survive. This non-virulent strain of blight appears to be spreading in the wild in American Chestnut trees in Connecticut and Michigan.

A gene that contains a tiny protein, which may afford a chestnut tree blight resistance, is being experimentally introduced into chestnut tissues in the laboratory. If the chestnut tissues grow normally in the presence of this gene, whole plants will be produced and field-tested for blight resistance. If these chestnut trees are indeed resistant, clones will be made available to the public through the State Nursery at Saratoga Springs!

AUSTRALIAN NOMADS CAMP
in the LIVINGROOM!

The most popular cage bird in the United States today is a tiny member of the parrot family, *Melopsitticus undulatus*, the budgerigar. Budgerigar is an anglicization of the Aboriginal word, "betcherrygah," meaning "good bird," as in good to eat!

The wild budgerigar, or budgie, is a small bird, measuring about seven inches from its head to the tip of its long, narrow tail. Its plumage is beautiful: a light, iridescent, grass-green on the chest and stomach, and black and yellow scallops on the head, shoulders and back. The forehead, face and neck are bright yellow, and there is a gay, purple-blue patch on each cheek. There are three black spots that look like upside-down valentines on each side of the throat. The swollen area around the nostrils, known as the "cere," is usually bright blue in a male bird and pinkish-tan in a female! The deep blue, tapering tail gives the bird an elegant silhouette.

Budgies have hooked bills, with the upper mandible curving down over the lower. Both portions of the bill are hinged, which makes it quite powerful and able to break open hard seeds. The bill also acts as a hand; it digs into the bark of a tree, affording the bird a good "grip" as it climbs about. All parrots have, on each foot, two toes pointing forward and two pointing backward. This enables them to grasp the branches tightly as they hang from them and swing acrobatically!

In the wild, flocks of budgies fly over the red sand deserts of Australia's interior, in a desperate search for water and food. When the rains come, just as in our American desert, dry creekbeds become rushing torrents and pools of drinkable water are filled. Soon, there is new plant growth all about—then flowers, then seeds. These seeds (primarily grass seeds) are the mainstay of the budgie's diet.

After a rainstorm, the loud, excited calls of budgies, back and forth across the hills, signal the sight of precious water. As they congregate, small flocks of thirty or forty birds join together to make flocks of hundreds or even thousands! The rains trigger a rapid breeding response in the birds, for now there will be enough food to raise babies.

Each pair of budgies seeks a hole in a tree—often a eucalyptus growing alongside a creek. Then, the female, with her strong bill, carves into the hole to create a nesting chamber within the tree. She lays up to eight, dull-white eggs placed on the wood chip floor of the nesting hollow. Her devoted mate brings her grass seeds to eat, all day long. After eighteen days, the babies hatch; after thirty days they are fully fledged and almost independent.

It is so important for the survival of the species that the budgies take full advantage of the presence of abundant food and water, that the female may start another clutch of eggs before the first babies are even fully fledged. Then, the father bird is very, very busy bringing enough food for the hen on the eggs and the first babies, all by himself!

The whole flock of budgies breeding together gives any individual bird greater safety from predators. The strident warning cries of a budgie who has sighted a predator, like a hawk, will cause the whole flock to scatter in every direction. Once the predator has gone, the birds' call-notes bring the flock together again.

When the rivers and pools dry up, and the plant life as well, the budgies must roam again in search of water. Just as their numbers increased dramatically in times of plenty, so do they now decrease in the time of thirst and starvation.

John Gould, the famous British naturalist, brought back some budgies from Australia to England in 1840. People were so enchanted by the vivacity, beauty, and intelligence of these charming little birds, that they imported them by the hundreds of thousands. They began to breed them as well. In 1875, the first yellow budgies were developed in Belgium. By the turn of the century, the number of budgies in the wild was so depleted that Australia enacted a strict embargo on their export. However, breeding programs were so successful in Europe that imported wild birds were no longer necessary. In 1910, the first sky-blue budgies were shown in Great Britain. Today, selective breeding has produced many beautiful new color variations, such as white, gray, violet, mauve and many shades of green and blue.

One of the most wonderful attributes of these tiny parrots is their ability to mimic sounds. I must confess that I am the happy owner of a sky-blue budgie who utters wolf whistles, speaks cheerful phrases, sings "After the Ball is Over," makes Guinea pig squeals, bell rings, and coughs when Edward has the flu!

THE EXQUISITE WOOD DUCK

In 1847, Thoreau wrote of the Wood Duck, "What an ornament to a river to see that glowing gem floating in contact with its water."

Where does one begin when trying to describe the appearance of this glorious bird? This tiny duck, only the size of a pigeon, is resplendent in the most beautiful plumage of any duck of North America. His brilliant green head bears a long sweeping crest, and his neck, back and tail feathers display many iridescent hues of green, purple and blue. He has a distinctive white throat, and a white collar and sideburns. His tiny bill is colored scarlet and white, trimmed with yellow and white, and his large eyes are ruby-red. His breast, the color of burgundy wine, is starred with white diamond flecks. His bronze flanks are barred with black and white, and he is white beneath.

The graceful female Wood Duck has a more gentle beauty. Her slightly crested head is sooty gray, her chin and throat are white, and she has a white, teardrop-shaped eye patch that bestows a constant anxious look upon her. Her basic body color is a soft, grayish-bronze with white dashes on her chest and sides. She too is white beneath. On the sides of her wings, she has some iridescent blue, purple and gold feathers. This lovely subtle coloration affords the hen good camouflage.

Wood Duck calls are very different from those of other ducks. The hen is quite obstreperous, producing a loud, squealing "wee-e-e-e-k" sound, especially when she is excited, but the drake can only softly whistle, "B-twee," similarly to a goldfinch.

Wood Ducks frequent wooded creeks, rivers, swamps and ponds, especially beaver ponds, from the Hudson Bay region of Canada to the Gulf of Mexico.

In this habitat, they dine on water plants such as algae, watermeal, milfoil, water-fern and duckweed, and eat the seeds of burr reed and arrow arum. They pick up mulberries that have fallen into the water or onto the ground, and fly amongst the trees where grapevines twine to pluck off grapes. They glean kernels of corn and wheat scattered in harvested fields. Wood Ducks actually prefer to eat acorns above any other food, and forage for them amidst the leaves beneath oak trees. Adult Wood Ducks are primarily vegetarian.

The Wood Duck is a true denizen of the forest. It flies easily between the trees on wings that are broader in proportion to its body size than those of other ducks. Its long rectangular tail acts as a rudder. Unlike most ducks, the Wood Duck is able to perch on branches and utilize tree cavities for nesting.

By early spring, most of the Wood Ducks will have paired off. The hens lead the quest for suitable nest sites. They have a good homing instinct, and will attempt to find the site that they successfully utilized the year before. They prefer a cavity in a tree that overhangs water. The holes made by Pileated Woodpeckers, thirty or forty feet on high, are often ideal.

The mother bird makes a depression in the rotted wood and plant litter within the hole. Here, she lays her twelve or so ivory-colored eggs. When she leaves the nest to feed, in the morning and again at sunset, she covers the eggs, first with litter, then with a blanket of down plucked from her breast.

While they are still in their shells, the mother duck calls softly to the babies, "kuk-kuk-kuk," and they answer her by peeping! After thirty days, the soft, silvery-gray ducklings hatch. When they are a day old, the mother duck waits below the tree, using that same call to urge her babies to fly down to her!

(Fortunately, baby Wood Ducks have very sharp claws on their webs, so they can clamber up the inside of their tree cavity to the opening.)

After the ducklings jump down to the water, their mother leads them to an area that is rich in high-protein food, such as insects, other invertebrates and tiny fish. This diet helps them to grow rapidly. After the ducklings are six weeks old, they become more and more vegetarian.

The ducklings are sometimes seized by hawks, or pulled under the water by bass, bullfrogs or snapping turtles. Wood Ducks are preyed upon by many other creatures, but their worst enemies are raccoons, followed by squirrels. They are taken by bobcats and opossums as well.

In late spring, the male Wood Duck begins to shed his bright feathers. He is then said to be in the "eclipse phase" and wears subtly-colored plumage, much like that of the female, that affords him camouflage. Because he has lost his flight feathers, he is extremely vulnerable to predators. Adult males in eclipse plumage retain their bright red eyes and bill, and can thus be distinguished from juveniles and females. (Juveniles resemble adult females but they are streaked with mottled brown rather than white.)

By autumn, the drakes have regained their flight feathers, and they and the females are clothed once again in their nuptial plumage. As the weather becomes colder, the time for migration approaches. Wood Ducks only travel far enough South to find open water with a good food source. Whereas, much of the year Wood Ducks appear in pairs and small flocks, in fall and winter they roost on the water, often in fresh water marshes, in flocks of hundreds!

At the turn of the last century, Wood Ducks became quite scarce due to unrestricted hunting. They were being shot for the table, and, because of their great beauty, for taxidermy. The passage in 1918 of the Migratory Bird Treaty Act between Canada and the United States saved the Wood Duck from extinction. Duck hunting in general would occur only from fall to early winter, and the Wood Duck could not be taken at all. By 1941, Wood Ducks had increased sufficiently so that one a season might be taken. Today, it is estimated that there are between seven and eight million of these glorious ducks flying in our skies!

A RECKLESS DEBAUCH

When one thinks of "salamander," one might visualize a sinuous and graceful creature like those crafted by jewelers as brooches in the Art Nouveau style. The appearance of our Eastern hellbender is very, very different. It is often described as grotesque, hideous, nightmarish!

The hellbender is a huge salamander, up to twenty-nine inches in length and five pounds in weight! It has a large, flat, bumpy head with tiny lidless eyes, and a long flattened body. Its legs are short and stout and its rudder-like tail is flattened vertically. The creature's color varies from gray to yellowish-brown to dark brown, with scattered dark spots on its back. Its skin is loose and wrinkly and there are wavy folds of skin that run down each side of its body and legs. Since the animal breathes through its skin, these folds afford it an increased surface area for respiration.

The hellbender's body form is well adapted to his life in chilly, swift-flowing streams with rapids and rocky bottoms. Crouched, hidden beneath a large flat rock or fallen tree in the shallows, he positions himself in the flow of a strong current and rocks slowly back and forth. This movement exposes all the surfaces of his skin folds to the oxygen-rich waters.

Salamanders often have picturesque names: newt, eft, siren, mudpuppy, waterdog, hellbender. *Webster's Dictionary* defines "hellbender" as "a reckless debauch." Perhaps our salamander's name refers to his voracious eating habits! All the day he rests quietly beneath his flat rock overhang, well camouflaged in his mottled wrinkly coat, but, come night, he goes forth eager to fill his large mouth with crayfish, minnows, tadpoles, worms and insects.

At four years of age, hellbenders mature. In New York State their courtship and breeding time begins in late August and extends through September. The hellbenders congregate in special breeding areas in shallow water where the males excavate large nest chambers beneath flat rocks.

A male hellbender will entice a female to enter his nest chamber, where she will lay several hundred eggs attached to one another in the manner of a long string of beads.

The male hellbender fertilizes the eggs then drives the female away. Now, he demonstrates his most admirable characteristic. He is a good, protective father! He guards the eggs faithfully for their incubation period of ten to twelve weeks.

The Eastern hellbender is listed as a "Federal Species at Risk." Its numbers continue to decline. It cannot lives in water whose quality has become so compromised that it can't support the hellbender's food sources. Because the hellbender breathes through its skin, it needs to be in clean, oxygen-rich water, unpolluted by sewage, industrial waste, or excessive silt due to damming, construction work or agricultural practices.

Many fishermen mistakenly believe that the hellbender is poisonous. When they catch one, they cut their line and the unfortunate creature is left to die with a hook in its mouth. If no such disaster befalls our hellbender, it may live out its totally aquatic life for over thirty years!

Today, the Eastern hellbender inhabits only two of New York State's river drainages—the Susquehanna and Alleghany River drainages and their associated tributaries. When a hellbender is discovered in a river from which it had long been absent, it is a newsworthy and cheering event, for it means that the river's health is improving!

A TINY WOODLAND ACROBAT

Now that the days are crisp and cool, and the trees are proudly displaying their glorious autumn hues, many of our feathered friends have left us to winter in warmer climes.

Those stalwart birds that remain to brighten our northern dooryards in the long, gray winter that approaches are all the more appreciated! One cheerful little visitor to the birdfeeder, often found in the company of his best friends, the chickadees, is the White-breasted Nuthatch.

He is a tiny bird, a little smaller than an English Sparrow. He wears a black cap that covers the nape of his neck, and his back is a blue-gray color. His dark slate wings are edged in black and his black tail feathers sport white bars. His face, throat and breast are white, shading to a light reddish hue beneath his tail.

Where the chickadee has a short, conical bill, the nuthatch has a long, narrow one; in fact, it is longer than his head! He uses this bill to probe beneath tree bark in search of ants, beetles, other insects and their eggs. In this manner, he helps to protect the trees from pests that would harm them in the spring. He hunts on the ground beneath the leaf litter for spiders, insects, and cocoons. If he finds a large insect, a nut or a seed, he snatches it, carries it to a tree and wedges it into a crevice in the rough bark. Then, he hacks and "hatchets" it with his strong bill till he breaks it open and extricates the meat within. Hence his name, "nuthatch!" Sometimes, he will leave a nut in a crevice, covering it with bark, when possible, in order to hide it from other hungry birds and eat it himself some later day.

Nuthatches, as well as their companions the Downy Woodpeckers, will greatly appreciate suet tied to a tree trunk in the winter. The nuthatch seizes a piece of suet, and, as though it were a large insect, presses it into the bark and hacks away at it with strong pecks.

The White-Breasted Nuthatch has a special ability that has earned him the name, "tree-mouse." He is able to run most rapidly up and down trees, always head first, and often, spiraling around the trunk. If the top side of a branch is covered with snow, he is able to run along the bottom side!

The nuthatches are able to perform these acrobatic feats because their toes and claws are very long and very strong. They climb a tree obliquely; they hang momentarily from the high foot and use the lower foot for support.

Most of the year, the call of the nuthatch is a simple, nasal *ank-ank-ank*, but in the spring, the male sings some musical notes as well. He and his mate can be heard twittering softly together, *wit, wit, wit.*

When it is time to nest, the nuthatches forsake our dooryards and retreat to the deep, cool woods. There, they seek a mature tree with a natural cavity, or, an abandoned woodpecker hole, fifteen to sixty feet above the ground. Both birds work together to line the cavity with bark shreds, twigs, grass, feathers, moss and even, rabbit fur. The male feeds the female while she sits on her clutch of eggs, usually eight in number. The beautiful, white eggs are heavily speckled at the large end with brown and lilac.

The affectionate nuthatch couple remains together after the breeding season; in fact, the pair bond may actually be permanent!

White-breasted Nuthatches can be found in mixed woodlands all over the eastern United States from Canada to the Gulf of Mexico, foraging happily in the company of Black-capped Chickadees, Downy Woodpeckers, Tufted Titmice and Kinglets.

The poet, Edith M. Thomas, captured the essence of our nuthatch thus:

Shrewd little haunter of woods all gray,
Whom I meet on my walk of a winter day—
You're busy inspecting each cranny and hole

In the ragged bark of yon hickory bole;
You intent on your task, and I on the law
Of your wonderful head and gymnastic claw!

The woodpecker well may despair of this feat–
Only the fly with you can compete!
So much is clear; but I fain would know
How you can so reckless and fearless go,
Head upward, head downward, all one to you,
Zenith and nadir the same in your view?

THE RETURN *of the* MOUNTAIN LION

On September 1, at about 8 a.m., an Accord couple, Andy and Debbie Lou Demskie, saw a large animal attack and kill one of their chickens. They believed that what they had witnessed was an attack by a mountain lion! The State Department of Environmental Conservation in our region receives about ten calls a year from people who are convinced that they have seen this most stealthy and elusive of creatures. These may be animals that have escaped or been released from captivity, or they may be of small colonies breeding in the wild!

When the settlers first arrived in America, the mountain lion, also known as the cougar, puma, panther, "painter" and catamount ranged over the entire country, from Canada to the Gulf of Mexico. Most people didn't want to live in proximity to these large, dangerous carnivores who had a penchant for killing livestock, such as, calves, colts, lambs and chickens, and bounties were placed on their heads. In Centre County, Pennsylvania, between the years 1820 to 1845, six-hundred mountain lions were killed for the bounty. By the late 1800s, mountain lions had been virtually exterminated from the Northeast, with the possible exception of a few remaining in the remote Adirondacks.

Today, with many old upstate New York farms returning to brushy fields and new growth forests, there is suitable habitat to support many small prey animals, such as rabbits, beavers, mice and porcupines. There is also much "browse" for the white-tailed deer, the northeastern mountain lion's favorite food!

This lion is a huge and dangerous predator. The male may be over eight feet in total length and weigh over two-hundred pounds; the female is somewhat smaller. Slender, lithe and very muscular, they are capable of springing fifteen feet upward or sixty feet downward!

They have the strength to drag heavy prey, such as a nine-hundred pound moose, for hundreds of feet across the snow.

An excellent climber, the mountain lion will often lie in wait on a rocky ledge or in a tree, then leap down on its victim, biting the neck and severing the spinal cord. Or, hidden, it may slink along after the prey, then pounce in the manner of a domestic cat hunting a field mouse!

If the lion doesn't eat all the prey at one time, it will cover the remains with leaves and sticks, and return for future meals.

Where mountain lions are commonly found today, for instance, in the Colorado Rockies, they have the uncomfortable habit of silently following after hikers. Several years ago, a young woman hiking in Boulder County, Colorado, was killed and eaten by a mountain lion. Fortunately, attacks by these lions on humans occur very rarely!

The eastern mountain lion is a very handsome creature. His thick fur, soft to the touch, is mostly a tawny golden-brown. He has a white chest and throat and buff underparts. HIs rounded ears stand erect, and his tail is heavy, long and with a dark tip. His face bears prominent whiskers and brownish stripes like mustachios around the muzzle. There is an all-black variety of eastern mountain lion found, today, mostly in Florida. One attribute of the mountain lion that is very disturbing to humans is the female's habit of producing blood curdling screams, often likened to those of a terrified woman, perhaps, being murdered! These screams often have to do with passionate interactions between male and female.

After a union with a male lion lasting for only several weeks, the female will chose a den site for her babies. It may be in dense brush, in a rocky crevice, or perhaps under a fallen tree. After a gestation period of three months, the babies are born—usually in the spring, but, possibly, at any time of year. Lion kittens are born blind but fully furred. Their light-brown coats are beautifully patterned with dark blotches, and their short tails bear dark rings.

The mother lion must be ever vigilant in protecting her babies from those that would harm them; even from their own father. When the kittens are two months old, they are able to go forth with their mother in nightly hunting trips. She will stay with them almost two years until they are self-sufficient, competent hunters.

People insist on building new homes high on the wooded hills, pushing out resident wildlife. Encounters with bears are no longer a novelty in the Woodstock area; in fact, some homeowners have nightly visits from bird-feeder seeking bears! Coyotes, once very rarely seen, are now seen frequently. People are dismayed to find that their free-roaming domestic cats are a favorite food of coyotes! The coyotes have multiplied here because there is much food for them. They are occupying the predator niche once filled by wolves and lions. If the mountain lion does return to inhabit this region once again, it will kill and eat the coyotes!

THE INSATIABLE SHORT-TAILED SHREW

Although short-tailed shrews are exceedingly common in the Northeast, many country dwelling people think they have never seen one. They mistake the small gray creature skittering through the leaves for a mouse!

The short-tailed shrew, known scientifically as Blarina, is about four inches long, and covered with silky, dense fur that can be brushed in either direction. He has small ears and minute eyes, almost hidden in fur. His eyesight is poor, but his senses of smell and of touch are acute. He has a very long, sensitive snout that he uses to probe in moist leaf litter and sniff out prey.

Although shrews are our smallest of mammals, they are ferocious. Because of their exceedingly high rates of respiration and heartbeat, their metabolic needs make them voraciously hungry, always! They must hunt by day and by night, in the most inclement weather, with no time to hibernate. Within a day, if three shrews are confined in a box, first, two will kill and eat the third, then, by nightfall, only one victor will remain—his stomach quite full!

Although classified as an insectivore, Blarina is opportunistic and enjoys a varied menu. His long probing nose discovers in the leaf mold: insects, earthworms, slugs, snails, centipedes, salamanders and carrion. He also eats vegetable matter—especially beech-nut kernels and seeds, some of which he may cache.

Even amongst shrews Blarina is unique. He has poisonous saliva! Woe to the young mouse noticed by voracious Blarina. He pounces on the hapless creature and bites it with his long, strong, hooked incisor teeth. Into the wounds flow the poisons whose effect is much like that of the cobra, and the mouse is paralyzed. Then he devours it with his numerous sharp teeth, tipped with red pigment. He can eat several times his own weight in a day!

Blarina has a gland on each side of his body that produces a strong odor, so disagreeable that some predators won't eat him. Birds don't have a good sense of smell, and owls, hawks and shrikes take him readily. He is also preyed upon by weasels, foxes, coyotes, wolves, bobcats, and house cats.

Blarina builds a spherical nest six to eight inches in diameter that incorporates dry grasses, shredded leaves, and, if available, rabbit hair. The entrance is a small opening on the side. Some shrews may shore up the edges of the nest with small stones! The nest may be built in a hollow tree, under a wood or brush pile, or in an abandoned mouse burrow. From spring to early fall, shrews may produce three litters with three to ten babies in each. The babies are born naked and helpless, and look like tiny, pink, wrinkled honey bees.

Within a month, the baby shrews are independent and are able to pursue their fierce, short lives. Because of their metabolic rate, most shrews "burn out" and survive less than one year!

THE SHY SERPENT
of OVERLOOK MOUNTAIN

One sultry July afternoon, a hiker climbs on the southern slope of Overlook Mountain. He pauses for breath, and notices movement in a pile of leaves directly before him. It is fortunate that he does not tread on that pile, for it hides a large, poisonous snake, the timber rattler!

The timber rattler's beautiful skin is patterned in such a way that it provides him excellent camouflage in the leaves. His back may be bright yellow, gray, or brown, marked with dark brown or black chevrons. Sometimes, his back and markings are so dark he appears to be almost black. He may be over six feet long, and he is stocky as well.

Timber rattlers inhabit heavily forested, mountainous terrain with cliffs, ledges, stone outcroppings and nearby streams. The forests are primarily deciduous hardwoods. When settlers came to the Woodstock area, they soon became aware of the rattlers inhabiting the eastern and southern escarpments extending from behind the village of Catskill to Phoenicia. Overlook Mountain in particular had great populations! The noted historian Alf Evers, in his wonderful book *Woodstock, A History of an American Town*, states "from the opening of the first Overlook Mountain House in 1871, the presence of timber rattlesnakes on the mountain caused nervous people to stay away.... Each spring men killed emerging snakes at the great den on top of 'The Minister's Face'... Jager's Cave on Overlook had a very determined concentration of rattlesnakes." Lewis Hollow, on the southern slope, was home to many of the creatures. Today, they are occasionally seen at California Quarry and Raycliffe.

Rattlesnakes are members of the pit viper family. They have flattened, triangular heads which are twice the width of their necks. They have a pit on each side of their face between the eye and the nostril. These pits can sense the radiant heat of an animal passing by and thus help the snake locate warm-blooded prey or predator, even in the dark!

The rattlesnake's eyes have pupils that are vertically elliptical. These eyes afford poor vision and primarily detect motion. There are no ear openings, but the creature senses vibrations in the ground with his whole body. These vibrations inform the snake of the size, distance, and direction of an animal passing nearby.

People are sometimes frightened by the sight of a snake flicking his forked tongue in and out of his mouth. The harmless tongue is actually gathering scent and taste particles from the air.

Our rattlesnake's scientific name, *Crotalus horridus*, means "horrid castanet." This refers to the creature's "rattle" at the end of its tail. The rattle consists of loosely attached horny segments, each of which originally covered the tail tip. Each time the snake sheds his skin (every year or two), these segments are not shed, but become part of the enlarging rattle!

When the snake senses a person's approach, it may slowly crawl away. If it feels threatened, it will coil and vibrate its rattle in the leaves. This produces a loud, insect-like buzzing which is a warning signal. Other snakes, such as the black rat snake or the milk snake, will rattle their tail tips in dry leaves to mimic the sound, hoping to be mistaken for the venomous rattler!

Rattlesnakes eat small mammals such as rabbits, squirrels, chipmunks, rats, mice and shrews. They will also eat birds and eggs. These snakes have venom which they pump from poison glands through hollow fangs into the unfortunate prey. Their upper and lower jaws are hinged in such a way that they can spread apart widely, and their lower jaws move apart sideways! Their teeth point backwards to their throats. Their body walls and skin have elasticity. These adaptations make it possible for rattlesnakes to swallow surprisingly large animals. After a meal, the snakes may not eat for weeks.

In the fall, the snakes congregate in the vicinity of their dens. These are located in wooded, rocky ledges with southern exposures. The snakes bask on the rocks in the warm autumn sunshine. By the colder days of winter, they have assembled within the dens, below the frost line, to hibernate. A den may hold over a hundred rattlesnakes, accompanied by copperheads and other snake species!

In the spring, the snakes emerge to bask and hunt for food. Being cold-blooded creatures, they are most active during the warm day. They mate, then begin to disperse throughout the woods. In summer, the snakes become more active at night. When there's a drought, they may descend to lower elevations than where they are usually encountered, following their prey.

The baby rattlers are born live, in late August to mid-September. They are enclosed in a transparent membrane which is shed within moments. Each baby is about a foot long. It is fully developed, with hollow fangs, venom, and a tiny rattle segment called a button!

Timber rattlers are themselves preyed upon by hawks, owls, raccoons, foxes and coyotes. Their populations are in a severe decline today due to indiscriminate killing by humans, illegal collecting for the pet trade, and loss of habitat to human development. They are classified as "threatened" in New York State and it is illegal to murder them.

If you would wish to see a timber rattler at first hand, attend the upcoming Dutchess County Fair. They are displayed there as an exhibit located in front of a menagerie.

A STARTLING BEAUTY

One sultry, summer afternoon, I stood on a grimy subway platform in Greenwich Village, in a throng of weary, hot commuters. One by one, as we became aware of an amazing sight, grim faces softened and smiles appeared. Right above our heads, floating in the dusty air, was a huge cecropia moth! What a splendid creature it was. It brought a moment of joyful wonderment to those jaded New Yorkers.

The cecropia is a member of the order Lepidoptera, and the family Saturniidae, our native giant silkworm moths. In fact, the cecropia is the largest moth in North America! Other members of this family are: the beautiful luna moth, the promethea moth, the polyphemus moth, and the io moth.

The caterpillars of the giant silkworm moths, although large, do not occur in sufficient numbers to cause extensive damage to the trees and shrubs they feed upon. Among these are the wild cherry, apple, plum, birch, maple, elderberry, lilac and willow; in fact, they dine on over fifty species of plants.

From a tiny white egg laid on the undersurface of a leaf, a tiny black larva emerges. It has six little feet near its head and many false feet as well, with which it can crawl along. It immediately begins the work of its life—to eat and eat, until its skin is so tight that it must split and be shed. The larva, or caterpillar, is now a dull orange color. When it outgrows its orange skin, it "molts" once more, and emerges as a yellow creature. The next molting produces a green caterpillar, decorated with rows of gaudy bumps, or tubercules—blue, red and yellow. After the next molt, the caterpillar has the same coloration. It gorges itself for two more weeks, and is, finally, more than three inches long. Now it is ready to make its cocoon.

The caterpillar spins a silken thread from its mouth, winds it many times about its body, and with it, attaches itself lengthwise to a twig. When the caterpillar is fully encased in its strong, well-camouflaged, brown cocoon, it becomes a "pupa." During this stage, the astonishing process of metamorphosis occurs. The body of the helpless pupa is changing from that of a caterpillar to that of a beautiful, winged moth.

In the spring, the adult moth, aided by two little hooks on either side of its body, pulls itself out through a weak spot at one end of the cocoon. Its large, velvety wings are crumpled and damp. The moth rests, then spreads its wings and pumps its body fluid through them. The wings expand, then dry. They are spectacular, five to six inches across!

The ground color of the wings is a rusty grayish-brown. Their outer margins are tawny in hue. The wings are crossed by white bands bordered in red, and each wing sports a white and red crescent near its center. Each of the upper wings has a red "eye-spot" near its apex. (Eye-spots on wings may be designed either to frighten off enemies, or conversely, to attract their attention away from the soft, vulnerable body.) The cecropia's furry body is reddish-orange with a white collar and white rings on the abdomen. The antennae resemble feathers.

The adult cecropia has mouth parts that are so undeveloped that it cannot eat. It lives just long enough to find its mate and reproduce. The male cecropia is attracted to a scent the female produces which he can perceive at a distance of three miles! After mating, the female has just enough strength to lay her tiny eggs, several hundred in number, and affix them to the undersurfaces of leaves. Both parents then die, but the emerging baby caterpillars continue the ancient cycle.

THE BEAUTIFUL BIRD *from the* WEST
WHO CAME TO STAY

I f you had lived in Woodstock, New York sixty years ago, you couldn't have had the pleasure of viewing the delightful house finch from your living room window. This charming little bird, then known as the California linnet, was native to Mexico, the western United States, and southwestern Canada.

In 1940, some unscrupulous people captured California linnets and shipped them to New York, to be sold illegally as cage birds, going by the name "Hollywood Finches." When the bird dealers in New York thought they were about to be arrested, they released the linnets into the wilds of Long Island.

There, they barely clung to life for a number of years, then finally, established a breeding colony. The descendants of these birds now occupy most of the eastern seaboard and are extending their populations ever westward toward their original range!

A house finch is a vivacious little bird, about the size of an English sparrow. The male bird has bright red feathers on his forehead, breast and rump. The rest of his upper parts are brown. His sides are pinkish-white, and his abdomen is white with brown streaks. His tail, legs and feet are brown. It is said that the most brightly colored males survive the winter better and more easily attract mates. (The beautiful red color is derived from carotenoid pigments that are obtained from the food the bird eats in the wild. The pigments are added to the feathers as they develop. When the house finch is kept in captivity, his red plumage may fade to a straw yellow.)

The house finch hen is modestly attired in a sparrow-like garb of grayish-brown with darker brown markings above, and white with dusky-brown streaks below.

House finches really enjoy living near people. They inhabit open woodlands and farms, but they are especially prevalent in cities and suburbs. They dine primarily on weed seeds, some occasional blossoms, buds and fruits, injurious insects such as plant lice, and, best of all, the seed offerings at bird feeders. They mingle there with chickadees, titmice, cardinals, nuthatches and goldfinches. They are bold and impetuous, but never aggressive like English sparrows!

It is such a delight to listen to the musical song of the house finch! It consists of a clear, sweet flow of warbling notes. This song is very similar to that of the house finch's close relative, our native purple finch. The purple finch, however, is much more shy, and not so apt to perform in the vicinity of a house.

In the spring, when it is time to choose a nest site, house finches may utilize a natural cavity low in a tree, a bush near a building, or even a vine on the side of a porch. The hen builds the nest herself. It is a shallow, well-made cup constructed of thin twigs, fine weed and grass stems, rootlets and leaves, and is lined with horsehair or feathers. Sometimes, instead of building a new nest, she may actually use a nest previously owned by other birds—even of other species!

The house finch hen lays four to six pale, greenish-blue eggs that are decorated with a few black speckles. As she incubates the eggs for about two weeks, the devoted male bird feeds her on the nest. The baby birds hatch out with bulging eyes closed and are helpless. Both parents then feed their down-covered young. The babies develop so rapidly that when they are ready to leave the nest in another two weeks, they are fully feathered in brown-streaked plumage and greatly resemble their mother. A pair of house finches may raise two or even three broods in a single season!

(At this time, some populations of house finches are being decimated by a contagious bacterial disease that causes partial blindness. The afflicted birds fly into obstacles and can't well elude predators such as cats. Unfortunately, the goldfinch is susceptible to this disease as well. Ornithologists at Cornell University advise the regular cleaning of bird feeders with a solution of one part bleach to nine parts water in order to kill these germs.)

A HAUNTING CALL *in the* GLOAMING

One evening last week, my friend DeeDee Halleck stopped by to tell me excitedly about the duck eggs she was attempting to hatch in an incubator. The night was sultry and all the windows were wide open. As we sat and chatted on the sofa, we became aware of the eery cry of a bird. Over and over came the mournful call: Whip-poor-WILL! Whip-poor-WILL! Whip-poor-WILL!

Our Whip-poor-will, *Caprimulgus vociferus*, is a member of the nightjar family of birds. In America, we say they are in the "goat-sucker" family, harking back to an old superstition that Whip-poor-wills could suck the milk from your goats!

Whip-poor-wills are plump birds about ten inches long, or the size of a jay. Because their habit is to rest all day amidst dry leaves on the ground, they have a protective coloration. The feathers on their upperparts are mottled brown, gray, tawny buff and black, and their barred and spotted underparts are similarly colored. The male birds also have a band of white feathers at the base of the neck and white patches on their tail feathers. The birds are rendered almost invisible in the dappled light filtering through the trees.

Whip-poor-wills have weak little toes and feet, so when they perch, they perch lengthwise along a low branch, crouched down and resembling a knot of wood!

When dusk falls, they rouse themselves and begin their repetitious, plaintive cries. Native Americans once believed these birds were the souls of their ancestors who had died in battle. Other superstitious people thought the birds had evil, occult powers. Actually, these birds are beneficial to man and catch myriad harmful insects.

The Whip-poor-will's bill is short and weak but its gape is very wide. The edges of the bill are furnished with feathers modified into stiff bristles. The bird makes numerous short hunting flights. Flying low over fields and streams with open mouth, he captures mosquitoes, June bugs, gnats and small moths. The whiskers around his mouth help entangle the prey. His long, velvety wings make him able to fly as silently as an owl.

Just before dawn, he begins to call again, but when the sun appears he falls silent. He returns to sleep in his preferred habitat: a glade surrounded by brushy, young hardwoods.

The mother Whip-poor-will lays her eggs, usually two in number, directly on well-drained ground, or perhaps, in a slight depression on a fallen log. As she sits on the eggs, her camouflage coloring makes her very hard to see in the surroundings.

The pretty eggs also have protective coloration. They are creamy white, overlaid with pale lilac-gray markings and brown splotches. The mother bird incubates the eggs for nineteen days. If she is disturbed on the nest, she may flap about pretending to have a broken wing, and draw away the intruder. Many people believe that a mother Whip-poor-will will move her eggs or young with her beak to a different spot if she perceives a threat, in the manner of a cat moving her kittens! (This idea, however, has never been proven.) Both parents feed their downy, yellowish-gray babies.

Because of their secretive, nocturnal ways, Whip-poor-wills are rarely noticed in migration. The Dutch settlers believed these birds had an uncanny ability to avoid being caught in a frost, so their arrival in New York in May meant there would be no more frost that spring. The birds make sure to leave New York in September, well before the first frost of fall. These warmth-loving creatures spend their winters as far south as Honduras!

GHOSTLY FLOWERS
of the SHADED FOREST FLOOR

On an early summer day in 1974, my husband Edward, our nine year old daughter Deirdre and I left lower Manhattan for a new life in the Catskills. Our first home in Lake Hill, a hamlet in the township of Woodstock, was on the old Sickler farm property. There were over twenty acres of pristine woods, a meadow and a creek to explore!

While Edward finished a manuscript, Deirdre and I set forth each day to discover the wonders of our natural surroundings. We would push through the high grasses of the wildflower-filled meadow (no fear of Lyme tick then) to the deep shade of the forest. One day in the woods, we came across something we had never seen before—a large patch of gleaming, ghostly Indian Pipe, a rare wildflower of the North. One never forgets the first encounter with this amazing life-form!

Indian Pipe is a true flowering plant furnished with nectar, pollen and seeds, but at first sight it looks more like a fungus. It is only four to ten inches high, translucent and a waxy, white color, sometimes compared to that of a corpse! Its leaves are reduced to scales. What we see, a stalk topped with a five-petalled flower, resembles a pipe whose stem is stuck in the ground. When the plant is ready to disperse its seeds, it straightens its bent head upward. This characteristic is described by its scientific name: *Monotropa uniflora*—meaning "once turned, one flower."

In order to appreciate Indian Pipe's niche in the plant community of the forest, we have to understand its relationship with a fungus, and the fungus's relationship with a tree.

A tree utilizes the chlorophyll in its great canopy of leaves to make sugar from CO_2 and water in the presence of sunlight.

A fungus puts out a network of filaments in the soil called hyphae, which utilize enzymes to break down rock and take up minerals.

These hyphae can also penetrate the roots of a tree, and transfer those useful minerals to it. In return, the hyphae obtain sugars to feed the fungus from those same tree roots!

Where does the Indian Pipe come into this nicely balanced equation? The Indian Pipe was once believed to be a saprophyte, or, a plant that lives off of decaying organic matter. Today, it is thought of as an "epiparasite," or a parasite upon a parasite! The Indian Pipe persuades the fungus, perhaps by copying chemical signals used by the tree, to penetrate its roots, and not only give it minerals, but also give it some of the sugars the fungus obtains from the tree! It is not known if the fungus obtains anything at all in return from the Indian Pipe.

Most of the time, the Indian Pipe lives underground as a mass of roots, feeding, but when it decides conditions are ripe for reproduction, often after a heavy summer rain, it sends up the ghostly flower. After pollination by an insect, the little flower produces thousands of very tiny seeds, which are dispersed on the wind. These seeds have no stored food. They lie in the ground waiting until they are penetrated by those fungal hyphae so that they can develop!

The Native Americans applied the sap of Indian Pipe on eye infections, and called it "eye bright;" the pioneers utilized the plant for nervous conditions and spasms, and called it "convulsion root." The plant is not used medicinally today because it is mildly toxic.

In studying Indian Pipe, one is impressed not only by this plant's unique strategy for survival but by the old lesson that species are interdependent in the web of life on our planet.

THE SKYDANCER

The American woodcock is a plump, short-legged bird of the sandpiper family—a shore bird that doesn't spend time at the beach! It is about the size of a quail, with rounded wings, a short tail, a short thick neck, and a very long, straight bill.

The woodcock's plumage has cryptic coloration, that is, it has a mottled pattern of rusty browns and grays that affords the bird good camouflage as it crouches during the day amidst fallen leaves. Male, female and fully feathered juvenile birds are all similar in appearance.

The woodcock is a crepuscular creature, that is, most of its feeding takes place at dawn or dusk. Its diet consists primarily of earthworms and insect larvae. The bird has a special adaptation to capture its prey. There are nerve endings in the lower third of its bill with which it can "feel" earthworms in the mud. Then, it can lift just the tip of the upper bill and seize the hapless worm! The underside of the upper bill and the tongue are rough and the slippery prey can be dragged out. The bill is thus both a probe and a forceps!

The woodcock's large, dark protruding eyes are set so high and so far back that it has overlapping fields of vision both in front and in back of its head. The woodcock can see above, behind and to the sides, as well as forward, while he is probing the mud for food, so that he can be aware of any predator intending to make a meal of him!

We find woodcocks inhabiting the edge of forests bordering moist meadows. They rest during the day, depending on their cryptically-colored plumage to conceal them. If one approaches them too closely, they shoot up explosively, their wings making a distinctive whistling sound.

The American woodcock is famous for its spectacular courtship "song flights" that occur in spring over the breeding grounds. These displays take place at dusk when the owls call, throughout moonlit nights, and at dawn.

At first, the male struts about in a clearing, calling a very soft "cook-ooo." Then, he begins to utter a repetitive, nasal "preent." He takes to the air, and in so doing, produces the whistling sound with his flight feathers. By a series of spiraling loops, he ascends to two or three hundred feet, and is sometimes lost to the observer in the dim light. Suddenly, he plummets earthward in a looping, slanting descent, singing "zleep, zleep" as he flies, and landing very near to where he took off!

(Since woodcocks don't possess gaudy feathers, they have developed the aerial displays to attract the attention and capture the approval of female birds.)

If the courtship display is pleasing to a female waiting nearby, the birds will mate, then, the hen will go forth to raise her family alone. Her nest is merely a slight depression she has scraped in the leaf litter on the ground, lined with grasses or pine needles and rimmed with twigs. Each day, she lays one buff-colored egg, decorated with light brown blotches and overlaid with darker brown markings. There are usually four eggs in all. She doesn't begin to incubate them till all are laid; that way, all will hatch at about the same time. When the hen is sitting on her eggs, she sometimes falls into a "brooding trance" and can actually be stroked by one who comes upon her!

After three weeks, the downy woodcock chicks hatch out, alert and with open eyes. Soon after hatching, they can follow their mother or crouch motionless at the approach of danger. In only two weeks, they can fly, and in four weeks, they are almost fully grown!

The American woodcock ranges in Eastern North America from Southern Canada to the Gulf of Mexico, however, the winters must be spent in the southern part of its range, for it must have unfrozen ground to probe for its food. When the days grows shorter, woodcocks assemble in loose flocks for their annual migration.

Unfortunately, woodcocks are heavily hunted game birds, prized for their flesh. Ed Sanders wrote in his biography of Chekhov in verse of an incident that took place when Chekhov and his friend Levitan went hunting woodcocks.

Levitan shot at a bird
which fell wounded
by his feet

"It had a long beak, large dark eyes,
and fine plumage."

It looked at the painter and writer
with astonishment

Levitan closed his eyes
and begged Doctor Chekhov,

"Kill it."

"I can't."

The bird continued its stunned stare.
Finally Chekhov killed it.

"One lovely, amorous creature less,"
he wrote,
"and two imbeciles went back home
and sat down to table."

COYOTE *the* TRICKSTER

One afternoon, several weeks ago, I looked out of my living room window and noticed three deer racing across my neighbor's apple orchard, their white tail-banners held high. I presumed they were being chased by dogs. Suddenly, a great scolding of crows broke out. I went behind the house to see what was causing the commotion and saw "it!" There, in the dappled forest light stood a strange creature—too big to be a fox, too small to be a wolf, and definitely not a dog. When it turned its wild gaze toward me, I realized I was looking at a coyote!

The name "coyote" is derived from an ancient Aztec word, "coyotl," which means "barking dog" as does the scientific name, *Canis latrans*. The coyote often begins his vocalization with high-pitched, staccato yips and barks, then leads into eerie wails and howls. These calls are often heard during the night and at the approach of dawn.

The ancient ancestors of the canine family of America, which includes wolves, foxes and coyotes, traveled back and forth across the land which once bridged the Bering Strait. A hare-eating coyote, *Canis leptophagus*, considered to be the ancestor of our modern coyote, returned to America two million years ago! Paleontologists have found the remains of coyotes in Native American campsites along the East Coast that are a thousand years old. The small wolf-like creatures described by early settlers in the East may have been coyotes.

The coyote is about four feet long from nose to tail tip, and usually weighs about thirty pounds. Its luxuriant fur is tawny in color, grizzled with gray, and ticked with black. The beautiful, very bushy tail is about sixteen inches in length. As the coyote lopes gracefully on its long, slender legs, the tail always droops low. The coyote has a "foxy" face, with a long pointed nose and large, erect, pointed ears.

The coyote's excellent senses of hearing and smell and its sharp eyesight help it to survive. It is thought of as being very intelligent, even crafty or tricky. Some Native American legends honor the coyote for its cunning. It can learn to recognize and avoid traps, and tell whether a man is carrying a rifle or not!

Unlike the wolf, the coyote does not form large, stable packs. He is either solitary, with his mate, or sometimes, in a small temporary group. Coyotes may pursue prey in relays. For example, knowing that a rabbit being chased by one coyote will run in a circle, a second coyote will sit and wait for its return, then it will be *his* turn to chase. Several coyotes will hunt a deer together by surrounding their quarry so that it will run around and around within their circle until it is exhausted. When a coyote attempts to catch a game bird, it will slink and creep through the grass, then pounce in the manner of a cat. The coyote may even play dead, and when a small creature comes close to investigate, he will leap up and seize it! Coyotes carefully choose their prey, picking out the sick, old, or weak animals. Domestic dogs, in contrast, will run in a pack through a herd, killing and maiming on every side.

Although classified as a carnivore, the coyote can thrive on almost any available food. He eats hares and rabbits, chipmunks and squirrels, mice and rats. He takes elk, antelope and deer fawns, turkey poults, and Canada geese. If he can get at them, he will eat sheep and goats. He eats insects, reptiles, fish, and in the winter, carrion. He likes juniper berries, rose hips, persimmons and watermelons. He is able to tell a ripe melon from a green one! The coyote can even eat grasses and sedges.

Coyotes actually benefit farmers by freeing their premises from injurious insects, rodents and rabbits. As one of the most important checks on the rodent population, coyotes can help prevent epidemics of diseases such as plague and Hanta.

Coyotes are said to choose a mate for life. When the breeding season arrives, in late January, a pair of coyotes seek out a den to house their coming family. They may utilize a natural cave or a cavity under a ledge, an abandoned burrow of, perhaps, a skunk or badger, a hollow log or even a patch of dense brush. If there is an abandoned burrow handy, they will enlarge it and form a long tunnel and a nesting chamber.

Just before the birth of the babies, the father departs to a separate home nearby. He brings food offerings and places them at the entrance to the nursery den.

After a gestation period of sixty-three days, the coyote pups are born. They are usually between five and ten in number. They are born blind and helpless, but covered with fur. After nine days, their eyes open! The mother weans the pups by regurgitating meat for them. When the babies are about two months old, the father is permitted to return, and he and the mother take the babies forth and teach them to hunt.

By late fall, the young coyotes begin to wander away and seek new territories of their own. Occasionally, some juveniles stay through the winter and help their parents raise a new litter!

The coyote today lives in a great variety of habitats: grasslands, deserts, woodlands, mountains and marshes. Although persecuted, it has expanded its range and is now found all over the United States—northward through Canada to Alaska, and southward to northern Central America. The extermination of wolves was an important factor in the coyote's expansion of range. When given the opportunity, wolves kill coyotes. In areas where wolves have been reintroduced, such as Yellowstone National Park, the coyotes' numbers have dwindled.

(Perhaps, those citizens of Woodstock calling for the extermination of our local coyotes might want to consider the reintroduction of wolves!)

THE SNOWBIRDS RETURN!

On the dreariest raw and blustery day of Autumn, a flock of tiny juncos, seemingly oblivious to the cold, will arrive at your dooryard feeder. The slate-colored juncos, now known as the dark-eyed juncos, are about the size of sparrows; in fact, they are actually members of the sparrow family. Their appearance is sometimes described poetically as "dark winter skies above and white snow below." Their heads, chests and backs are deep gray, their underparts a soft grayish-white, and their tails, gray with clear white edges. When startled, the juncos leap into flight, their spread tails flashing white "V"s. Some believe they are signaling to their relatives, showing the way to follow!

With their strong, pink beaks, the juncos are well-equipped to glean the cracked corn and sunflower seeds that other birds cast out of your feeder to the ground. If you don't have a feeder, they will dine on your weed seeds, such as those of crabgrass and ragweed. The juncos, in their sober, gray suits with white trim, look like tiny feathered Pilgrims at a Thanksgiving feast! (In warm weather, juncos enjoy an occasional berry, and eat harmful insects, such as, caterpillars, grasshoppers and ants. From our point of view, they are exemplary birds!)

The congenial juncos are quite sociable, and are found in flocks of from ten to thirty individuals. They also fly in mixed foraging flocks, accompanying chickadees, white-throated sparrows, white-breasted nuthatches, golden-crowned kinglets, and downy woodpeckers.

Juncos seem unfazed by the coldest weather. They may even be seen bathing in powdery snow! How do they maintain a body temperature of over a hundred degrees when the cold winds blow? Near their skin, there is a layer of down feathers that trap and retain body heat. Over these, there are tightly overlapping outer feathers which the birds spread with oil taken from a special gland. These oiled outer feathers act as a shield to keep warmth in and rain and wind out.

When the birds perch, they stand first on one foot and then on the other, so that four toes are always drawn up into their warm belly feathers. Juncos like to sleep in a dense evergreen, or, on a very cold night, they may even burrow into a haystack!

Sometime in April, the little snowbirds leave us to return to their cool, woodland breeding grounds high in the mountains of the U.S., in the northern parts of the states which border Canada, and in all of Canada and Alaska. The male birds arrive first and stake out their territories. The female birds arrive a few weeks later and choose their mates.

Besides his usual low, twittering call, the male junco now sings a soft, musical, trilling song. The female chooses a mate by considering the appeal of his song, the suitability of his territory as a nesting site, and his overall appearance and élan!

After an elaborate courtship ritual, the birds build their nest in a surprising place—on or very near to the ground! A favorite site is under the upturned roots of a tree. Sometimes, the nest is well-concealed on a grassy slope or under the overhang of a mossy bank.

The nest is a carefully constructed, deep cup woven of grasses, moss, rootlets, twigs and strips of bark, and it is lined with finer grasses and hair. The eggs are four to five in number. They are pale bluish-white, and beautifully decorated with spots and blotches of brown, purple or gray, concentrated at their larger ends.

The mother bird incubates the eggs for thirteen days. When the babies hatch out, they are altricial, that is, helpless, naked and blind. When they obtain their juvenile plumage, it is streaked as is that of other sparrows.

Should a predator threaten the little family, the valiant mother bird will flutter along the ground with wings outspread, hoping to divert its attention from the nest. Those baby birds that survive to reach adulthood will join their friendly junco relatives and return to our dooryards to cheer our winter days once again!

SMALLEST SONGSTERS *of* SPRINGTIME

Ere yet the earliest warbler wakes, of coming spring to tell,
From every marsh a chorus breaks, a choir invisible,
As if the blossoms underground a breath of utterance had found.
                                             —TABB

One night last week, when the weather was astonishingly warm for March, I went out with my new friend Judy to listen to the Spring Peepers. We drove to Hurley, parked by the side of the road, and walked into a wet field. At first, we walked through grasses and weeds, then, pushed our way through brambles until the brush was higher than our heads and the ground was criss-crossed with tiny rivulets. Faintly, in the distance, we could hear the ugly whooshing of tires on pavement, but in the shrubs all around us an ancient song rose loud and glorious. It was a chorus of clear, musical ascending whistles in a complex interaction of calls and answers, produced by the tiny tree frogs known as Spring Peepers.

Tree frogs are not true frogs, but are closely related to toads. They are placed in their own family known as Hylidae. The Spring Peeper, *Hyla Crucifer*, is such a dainty, charming creature, only three-fourths of an inch to one and one-fourth inches in length. It is light brown or gray, and carries a dark, diagonal Greek cross (St. Andrew's cross) on its back. It has dark stripes on its long hind legs.

The Peeper has an amazing ability. Within a half-hour, it can change its skin color to match its surroundings! The dark lines that form the cross on its back change to blotches which give a mottled effect and provide excellent camouflage. The Peeper sleeps during the day, and is very hard to spot clinging to the bark of a tree with its specially adapted toes. Each toe-tip has an adhesive disc by means of which the Peeper can climb up slippery vertical surfaces—even the sides of a glass terrarium!

All tree frogs are carnivores. The Peepers dine primarily on small spiders or insects. Their tongues are fastened at the front of their mouths, not at the back as ours are. They can "shoot out" their tongues to catch insects, and will even jump in the air to snatch their prey. They can jump a distance over seventeen times their body length! When they swallow, they blink, which presses their bulging eyes downward and helps push the food down from mouth to stomach.

The surprisingly loud song of the tiny Peeper is produced by courting males. They enormously inflate their vocal sacs with air. When the sacs are filled with air, they become sounding boxes for the noises produced by the vocal cords. Some people think that Spring Peepers heard at a distance sound like sleigh bells!

The females lay eight hundred to one thousand eggs, each in its own globule of jelly and affixed singly to stems and stones in the water; the male then fertilizes them. The tiny tadpoles are a metallic reddish color. It takes about three months for them to develop into "froglets." Curiously, they leave the water while they still have their tails! By fall, the little Peepers have eaten a great deal and stored food in their bodies anticipating hibernation. Sometime in November, when the weather becomes truly cold, they hibernate— beneath moss, leaves, loose bark, or perhaps, under a log.

Spring Peepers are found in woods surrounding ponds and swamps, ranging from South East Canada southward to Central Florida, and westward to Texas.

There has been a world-wide decline in the populations of certain amphibia. There are several reasons for this; a major one being the destruction of wetlands which are their breeding grounds. Automobiles take a huge toll of the tiny creatures hopping across the rain-wet roads at night. Those that avoid being crushed may meet concrete road dividers that prevent migration to their ancestral ponds. Some scientists suggest that the damaged ozone layer in the upper atmosphere allows through too much harmful ultraviolet

B light that strikes and harms the eggs. It is certainly true that amphibians absorb gases and chemicals easily through their skins, and the absence of these animals in a wetlands is a good indicator that pollution is present. Let us hope that our wonderful Peepers, harbingers of spring like the Robins and Bluebirds, will always remain plentiful in our region!

A PLANTER *of* FORESTS

The eastern gray squirrel, *Sciurus carolinensis*, is a large, intelligent, interesting rodent. He has smooth, silvery fur, and a beautiful fluffy tail which floats gracefully as he runs and leaps. This tail has several purposes. The squirrel can communicate that there is danger by flashing it while giving an alarm call. It helps him keep his balance as he jumps from branch to branch. If the squirrel falls, the tail acts as a parachute. It is a blanket wrapped around him in the winter nest, and, held curved over his back, an umbrella in the rain.

The squirrel expresses his emotions with a number of calls— chattering, chirping, scolding and squealing. He even stamps his feet when upset!

Squirrels charm us as they sit up to eat, holding in their front paws their pine cones and beechnuts, seeds, hazelnuts, acorns and hickory nuts. Each fall, when we watch squirrels burying their nuts for winter, we wonder if they will ever be able to find them again.

Squirrels actually have very keen senses. Their sense of smell is so acute that they are able to locate nuts buried under several inches of snow and earth. (Some nuts, however, are never retrieved. These may take root and grow into valuable forest trees that will provide food for the squirrels' descendents.) Squirrels' large bright eyes, placed on the sides of their heads, allow them to see in all directions. Their hearing ability is excellent as well.

In the autumn, gray squirrels compete with red squirrels and red-headed woodpeckers for the nuts still hanging on the trees. A woodpecker determined to have a nut will beat the squirrel with his sharp bill until the squirrel retreats!

Red-tailed hawks are the squirrels' true bird enemies. Red-tails sometimes hunt in pairs, and when they pursue a gray squirrel, it has little chance to save its life. Gray squirrels are also preyed upon by tree-climbing snakes, foxes and bobcats.

A squirrel prefers to build its winter home in the hollow of a maple, birch or beech tree, with the entrance forty to sixty feet above the ground. The nest hole is insulated with leaves, grasses and other soft materials. The summer nest resembles that of a crow when seen from below. It is a bulky creation of sticks, bark and leaves, lined with grass. The entrance is on the side, near the trunk of the tree.

There may be three nests for each squirrel family: one for the male, one for the mother and her babies, and one for the immature offspring of the previous litter.

In late February through April, in the North, the gray squirrel babies are born. The tiny creatures are helpless and naked, with closed eyes and ears. After two months, they are able to climb about on their home tree. The mother squirrel is devoted and affectionate, and the babies often stay with her throughout their first winter. Sometimes, the mother squirrel will move her babies to a fresh clean nest. She does this by carrying each baby in her mouth, while it wraps its feet around her head and neck!

Unlike other members of the squirrel family, such as the chipmunk or woodchuck, the gray squirrel does not hibernate. On the most inclement days, it stays in its nest with its fluffy tail wrapped around its body, perhaps, snuggled up to other squirrels for warmth. In fact, up to thirteen male squirrels have been found living cosily in one nest!

Some years, the squirrel mortality along the roadway is tremendous. Scientists think that this occurs when there is an overpopulation of squirrels. They go forth in a desperate search for food and water. Squirrels undertook gigantic migrations across the countryside in pioneer days. Hundreds of thousands of squirrels swam lakes, and drowned in rivers such as the Hudson and the Ohio. As the squirrels pushed forward, they destroyed every corn and wheat field in their path.

In the book, *Speaking of Animals*, Alan Devoe describes one of these mass migrations. "On a three-day hunt in Ohio, in 1822, the gray squirrels taken were 19,660. Migrating from area to area, in the fall of the year, squirrels traveled in gatherings estimated to contain nearly a quarter of a million. There are records, not to be disputed, of bands of squirrels advancing along fronts a hundred miles wide, and requiring five days to pass."

In 1842, in southeastern Wisconsin, a great migration occurred that lasted four weeks. The renowned naturalist, Seton, estimated that it may have contained half a billion squirrels! According to Seton, the last of these great treks occurred in 1866. Squirrels today still have mass migrations, but they are usually composed of hundreds of individuals instead of thousands.

The eastern gray squirrel may be found in its favorite habitat, a deciduous hardwood forest with nut trees, a suburban back yard or even a city park. They range from southern Canada southward along the Eastern Seaboard to Florida, and westward to the Plains States. They have even become established in Europe!

LOST *and* GONE FOREVER

Wouldn't it be delightful to look out of a window one summer day and see a flock of beautifully-colored parakeets, native to our own area? If this were the end of the nineteenth century, and not the beginning of the twenty-first, we could have! The Carolina parakeet, a small member of the parrot family, about the size of the mourning dove, once ranged up and down the East coast, from Florida to the Great Lakes. In fact, it was the only parrot native to the United States.

What a wonderful bird this was! It was about twelve inches in length, including its long, slender tail, and clothed in iridescent, light green feathers. Its wings were bordered with olive and gold and its golden neck shaded to a glowing orange face and head. Its pinkish-brown feet, like those of all parrots, had two toes pointing forward and two pointing backward, allowing it to grip the branches as it climbed about them. The upper and lower sections of its large, hooked bill were both mobile, to afford it great strength for the cracking open of hard-shelled seeds, while its thick, flexible tongue extracted the kernels. The humble cocklebur was the mainstay of its diet, and it also enjoyed the occasional wild fruit.

The Carolina parakeet inhabited swamp-filled woodlands such as those of Woodstock and Saugerties. It would seek out a tree cavity and enlarge it in the manner of a woodpecker for a nesting site. Out of several tiny, white eggs would hatch the baby parakeets, naked, blind and helpless. Both doting parents shared in the care of the babies, feeding them on regurgitated seeds.

As do all members of the parrot family, the Carolina parakeets formed life-long, loving bonds between mates and companions. Unfortunately, this noble characteristic aided in their destruction!

By the nineteenth century, the fashion of hats laden with wild bird feathers became so extreme that some hats were actually decorated with entire stuffed birds! Thousands of parakeets were murdered for their gorgeous feathers. At the same time, more and more wet woodlands were converted to crop fields and orchards. The parakeets pecked the apples and pears, and enjoyed the new grains. They even swarmed over haystacks, picking out the nutritious seed heads. Then, the wholesale slaughter began.

Enraged farmers blasted the little birds with shotguns, killing perhaps twenty at a time. Those birds, terrified but not hit, first flew away, then returned to hover and shriek in despair over their fallen comrades. The farmers shot again and again, wiping out whole flocks at a time.

Over a period of about ninety years, the number of Carolina parakeets dwindled until flocks were no longer composed of a hundred birds, but rather, several birds or a pair. Realizing that the birds were on their way to extinction, hunters trapped them to sell to zoos, or shot them so that their skins could be sold to museums or universities. The last sure sighting of Carolina parakeets in the wild took place in April of 1904. The famous ornithologist, Fred Chapman, observed thirteen birds in Florida, near Lake Okeechobee.

In the meantime, one pair of Carolina parakeets remained in the Cincinnati Zoo. When the female bird, "Lady Jane," died, her cage mate of thirty-two years, "Incas," fell into a decline. His keepers at the Zoo insisted that he was mourning his lost mate. In February of 1918, the last Carolina parakeet vanished from this earth.

There is an interesting corollary to this story. In the nineteen-sixties, it is thought that a shipment of South American Monk parakeets, also known as Quaker parakeets for their coat of conservative gray and green feathers, escaped from Kennedy Airport. Colonies of these birds, of the same size and of similar disposition to our Carolina parakeet, are now encountered in southeastern New York, New Jersey, Connecticut, Massachusetts, Virginia and Florida. The parakeets prefer to live in suburbia, where they delight the community when they visit bird feeders. They differ in one way from all other parrots: they build bulky, large, communal nests of twigs, clearly visible in a tree or on a utility pole.

The Monk parakeet has never been shown to have any detrimental effects whatsoever on the environment in the United States. So determined are the authorities that we not have these parrots in the wild, and knowing that they can't shoot them near people's homes, they smash down the conspicuous nests, killing the eggs and babies within. Some states in the northeast permit Monk parakeets as caged birds; others do not. The law in Pennsylvania is this—if the authorities are made aware that a person has a pet Monk parakeet, perhaps legally purchased in New York, they may seize the bird and destroy it as if it were a rabid raccoon!

There are only a few parrot species that are able to live in temperate climates. The thick-billed parrot is one. It is a stocky, green bird about fifteen inches in length. Its forehead, the bend of the wing and the thighs are bright red. The underwing has a bright yellow patch, visible in flight; the strong bill is black and there is a bare yellow ring around the eye.

In the 1700s, huge flocks of these birds ranged from the western United States to Venezuela. They would make yearly migrations from Mexico into the high pine-oak forests of Arizona and New Mexico, where they ate piñon nuts, agave flowers, wild fruits and acorns. By the 1930s, they had been exterminated in the United States due to wanton hunting for "sport" and feathers.

In 1987, our government released twenty-nine thick-billed parrots in the Chiricahua Mountains of Arizona. Money was raised by zoos, wildlife organizations, bird clubs and school children here and abroad to study these birds and monitor their survival. The project was, at first, considered to be a success, but this flock and subsequent releases of birds were decimated by disease and predation by hawks. At this time, no further releases are planned. The thick-billed parrot is highly endangered in its remaining range due to hunting, loss of habitat, and loss of nesting sites.

Let us hope these beautiful birds don't follow their cousins, the Carolina parakeets, into oblivion!

About the Author

MIRIAM SANDERS is a naturalist, a writer, a painter and illustrator, and an environmentalist who has lived more than 40 years in Woodstock, NY. She is the author and illustrator of *Marie in the Moonlight*, the story of the nighttime adventures of a mouse on Meads Mountain in Woodstock.

For over ten years, Miriam Sanders has helped produce the Woodstock Journal, a weekly Public Access television program in Woodstock.